ALSO BY MICHAEL KINSLEY

Please Don't Remain Calm: Provocations and Commentaries

The Best of Slate: A 10th Anniversary Anthology

Big Babies: Vintage Whines

Curse of the Giant Muffins and Other Washington Maladies

CREATIVE CAPITALISM

A CONVERSATION WITH
BILL GATES, WARREN BUFFETT,
AND OTHER ECONOMIC LEADERS

Edited by **Michael Kinsley** with **Conor Clarke**

WITH CONTRIBUTIONS FROM:

Abhijit Banerjee • Gary Becker • Jagdish Bhagwati • Nancy Birdsall • Matthew Bishop • Warren Buffett • Kyle Chauvin • Gregory Clark • Clive Crook • Josh Daniel • Brad DeLong • Michael Deich • Esther Duflo • William Easterly • Justin Fox • Alexander Friedman • Milton Friedman • Bill Gates • Ronald Gilson • Ed Glaeser • Tim Harford • Nancy Koehn • Michael Kremer • Steven Landsburg • Thierry Lefebvre • Loretta Michaels • Matt Miller • Paul Ormerod • Edmund Phelps • Richard Posner • John Quiggin • Robert Reich • John Roemer • Vernon Smith • Elizabeth Stuart • Lawrence Summers • David Vogel • Eric Werker • Tracy Williams • John Williamson • Martin Wolf

SIMON & SCHUSTER

New York   London   Toronto   Sydney

Simon & Schuster
1230 Avenue of the Americas
New York, NY 10020

First Simon & Schuster hardcover edition December 2008

SIMON & SCHUSTER and colophon are registered trademarks
of Simon & Schuster, Inc.

For information about special discounts for bulk purchases,
please contact Simon & Schuster Special Sales at 1-800-456-6798
or business@simonandschuster.com.

Designed by Jaime Putorti

Manufactured in the United States of America

10 9 8 7 6 5 4 3 2 1

Library of Congress Cataloging-in-Publication Data

Creative capitalism : a conversation with Bill Gates, Warren Buffett, and
other Economic Leaders / edited by Michael Kinsley with Conor Clarke ;
with contributions from Abhijit Banerjee . . . [et al.].
    p.   cm.
   1. Capitalism.   I. Kinsley, Michael E.   II. Clarke, Conor.
III. Banerjee, Abhijit V.
   HB501.C7854   2008
   330.12'2—dc22   2008038977

ISBN-13: 978-1-4165-9941-8
ISBN-10:   1-4165-9941-X

ACKNOWLEDGMENTS

Three people are primarily responsible for putting this book together. One is me, and I bear ultimate responsibility for the content. One is Kyle Chauvin, a Harvard junior and protégé of one of our most loyal participants, Professor Ed Glaeser. Kyle won me over when he sent a résumé apologizing that he was only partially fluent in Mandarin Chinese. And one is Conor Clarke, now with the *Atlantic Monthly,* who started out as a research assistant and ended up as coeditor. I'm still not sure how that happened, but I'm glad that it did.

Several bloggers were kind enough to help us get the word out about the book's website, and we are grateful to them. They include Ian Ayres, David Brewster, Tyler Cowen, Ezra Klein, Arnold Kling, Nick Kristof, Steven Levitt, Greg Mankiw, Megan McArdle, Nico Pitney and the Huffington Post, Reihan Salam, Chris Suellentrop, and Matthew Yglesias. Thanks as well to our editor, Priscilla Painton at Simon & Schuster, and to my literary agent, Rafe Sagalyn, creative capitalists both.

CONTENTS

CONTENTS

CONTENTS

CONTENTS

CONTENTS

CONTENTS

CONTENTS

CREATIVE
CAPITALISM

INTRODUCTION
Michael Kinsley

This is a book about the possibility of expanding capitalism into new areas and using it to solve problems that previously were assigned to charity or to government. The timing is not great. As I write at the end of September 2008, we are in a financial crisis, the dimensions of which are still uncertain. It's safe to say that if capitalism were a stock and reputation were a currency, the stock has plummeted in the past couple of weeks. As recently as Labor Day, that stock was still soaring, and people were talking about capitalism's unfulfilled potential and were full of ideas (some of them discussed in this book) for using markets in creative new ways. Now the notion of letting capitalism loose seems as appealing as letting loose a pack of rabid dogs. Maybe by the time you read this, it will all be over or turn out to have been media-induced panic.

Or maybe not. If economic catastrophe lies ahead, some of the contributors to this book will undoubtedly be saying that we should be much better off if only corporate America had stuck to its knitting. But whatever develops, nothing is likely to under-mine the general worldwide consensus that free-market capitalism (to borrow from Churchill) is the worst economic system except for all the others. And if we're in for a rough patch, we will be especially glad that the past few years have imbued corporations with a greater sense of social responsibility.

Indeed, everyone wants to Do Good these days, from college students to Hollywood actors to New York socialites to corporate CEOs. It's far from clear how much good this will do. Nevertheless, it is a trend that should be encouraged, don't you think?

But there are problems. The fad for doing good among big corporations is especially problematic, since corporations are fictitious entities that exist, by special dispensation of the law, for the specific purpose of pursuing the group self-interest of the shareholders. Yet corporations so completely dominate our economic landscape that if they are not included somehow in the great good-for-all, it isn't likely to amount to much.

In January 2008, Bill Gates gave a speech at the annual hoo-hah in Davos, Switzerland, known as the World Economic Forum. The most successful capitalist of all time—if successful capitalism is measured in dollars (have you got a better measure?)—Gates was planning to resign his corporate post and devote most of his time to the Bill & Melinda Gates Foundation, which he and his wife had founded several years earlier. A good case can be made that the years since the foundation's birth had already turned Gates into the greatest philanthropist of all time as well. Certainly, this is true if success in philanthropy is measured in dollars. By 2008, the Gateses had donated more than $30 billion to their foundation, and the foundation had given away more than $16 billion. What's more, Gates's friend Warren Buffett had decided to make the Gates Foundation the vehicle for giving away most of his own fortune, thus increasing the foundation's assets to the equivalent of more than $60 billion. (Technically, Buffett hasn't turned over his pile yet and won't until he dies. Instead, he gives the foundation 5 percent a year and requires that all of it be spent. Since the law requires foundations to pay out 5 percent of their assets every year, this has the same effect as if Buffett had given the foundation another $30 billion.)

However, just as money is only one measure of Gates's success as a capitalist, it is also only one measure of his success as a philanthropist. The discipline and focus he has brought to his giving is another measure, along with his insistence, against what must be constant pressure from fellow business executives with pet causes, that poverty and disease in faraway lands are more urgent than the local opera company.

Another measure of Gates's success as a philanthropist would have to be the reversal of his own popular image. Some have suggested that this was his motive all along, which is ridiculous. Nobody spends $30 billion on a PR campaign. But five years ago, he was widely perceived as an evil monopolist. A movie, with the unriveting title *Antitrust,* even portrayed him as a murderer. Today the name Bill Gates evokes philanthropy rather than sharp business practices. This isn't the first such transformation. John D. Rockefeller and Andrew Carnegie did something similar.

Gates had been rich, if not mega-rich, for twenty years or so before he started engaging in philanthropy to any significant degree. He took a lot of heat for not starting earlier, but he always said that giving away money requires as much thought as making money and that he would turn to the latter when he was through with the former. And, to the surprise of some, that is what he has done. Microsoft under Bill Gates was not a company known for its soft edges. In his Davos speech, however, Gates advocated a different approach. He called it "creative capitalism." What exactly he meant by that term was not clear, and indeed trying to parse the phrase is one of the themes of this book. One way or another, it meant that the big, increasingly global corporations that are the distinguishing feature of modern capitalism should integrate doing good into the way they do business.

How to combine the good life in the moral sense with a good life in the material sense is a question faced by real people as well as by corporations. After Bill's speech, I toyed with the idea of trying to write a book about creative capitalism or edit a collection of essays on the topic by people who might know more about it than I did. Then I had what I hope was a better idea. This book is a test of that idea. It's a literary experiment.

For seven years (from 1995 to 2002), I worked for Microsoft. My job was to start a "webzine," now an antiquated term. That was the online magazine Slate (slate.com) which today is owned and published by the Washington Post Company. It's hard to believe now, when computer screens are destroying the newspaper industry, but then there was skepticism that people would read anything voluntarily—that is, not work-related—on a screen. Even today, there are still a few forms of writing that resists computers, and that is long-form journalism or fiction.

At a meeting at Microsoft before Slate had begun publication, we were wondering how long an article we could expect people to read on a screen, when someone said, "But people will read thousands and thousands of words of email at one sitting." At the time, Microsoft was at the leading edge of the tidal wave of email that was about to engulf practically everyone in advanced societies. People complain about it, but many do read thousands of words of email every day and would miss it if it disappeared. Now there is texting and there are blogs and RSS feeds as well.

The force noted by that Microsoft exec (I am pretty sure it was Nathan Myrhvold) that impels us to read words of email by the thousands has its parallel in writing. Can there be any doubt that the number of words the world produces has skyrocketed since computers became linked? Yes, I know that joke too: it's not writing, it's typing. But some of it is not bad. Some of it, in fact, is good. What's more, it's easy—or at least it's easier than "real" writing. Many professional writers who think they find writing painful and consider it a lucky day if they produce five hundred words, can sit down and grind out half a dozen eloquent emails adding up to ten times that amount.

We can debate the quality of internet prose: the suspension of grammar, the cutesy acronyms (not to mention emoticons!), the casual spelling, the half-finished sentences, but it is the language of our time. And people do read it. And write it.

So the idea for this book was to find a collection of smart people, entice them into a web-based discussion of creative capitalism, and by this means trick them into producing a book. The book would have the quality of a blog or a "chat" or one of Slate's email dialogues. The prose would be casual, the organization perhaps a bit chaotic. The experience of "reading" it would be somewhat like surfing the web—except without hyperlinks.

Plenty of books have grown out of websites. But have there been websites started with the specific intention of using them to produce a book? Maybe, but not many. This method of producing a book may remind you of the way Tom Sawyer got Aunt Polly's fence whitewashed. But rest assured that the contributors will be compensated. The book's advance—minus expenses—was divided by the number of words ultimately published. This method—which balances incentives for quantity and quality—was intended to impress and entice economists.

At the beginning of this project, we made a key, and really stupid, mistake. Ignoring everything that the world has learned in the past couple of decades about openness and transparency on the web, we began by building a website and closing it off, requiring a password to get in. We thought that big-shot economists and others would be more likely to join and contribute if this was something exclusive. Not only snob appeal was involved. There was the ever-present concern that a Gary Becker or a Larry Summers would find himself brutally, or even obscenely, insulted by one of the many nuts who seem to spend their lives hanging around parts of cyberspace where they don't belong, determined to make serious participants miserable. This has been my experience at every website I have ever been involved with.

Until now. When we started trying to sign up our dream list of distinguished economists, we generally found that it was easy to evoke promises of participation from them but harder to actually get the goods. Economists, like everybody else, have short time horizons. Their desire to not be harassed by us in the short run—and possibly a genuine interest in the project— led them to say yes, but the longer run—in which they would actually have to write something—never seemed to arrive.

So, with some trepidation, we decided to go public. We simplified what had been an elegant but complicated site into a simple public blog, using the well-known blogging software TypePad. The results were remarkable. Suddenly we were generating thousands of pageviews of traffic every day, other blogs were shilling for us, and long-promised contributions were actually materializing. It seems that even distinguished economics professors like to be told, "Hey, I saw your piece." They like it even more than being in an exclusive club with other distinguished economics professors.

A NEW APPROACH TO CAPITALISM

Bill Gates

(Remarks delivered at the World Economic Forum,
January 24, 2008, in Davos, Switzerland)

This is the last time I will come to Davos as a full-time employee of Microsoft.

Some of us are lucky enough to arrive at moments in life where we can pause, reflect on our work, and say: "This is great. It's fun, exciting, and useful—I could do this forever."

But the passing of time forces each of us to take stock and ask: What have I accomplished so far? What do I still want to accomplish?

Thirty years, twenty years, ten years ago, my focus was totally on how the magic of software could change the world.

I believed that breakthroughs in technology could solve the key problems. And they do—increasingly—for billions of people.

But breakthroughs change lives only where people can afford to buy them—only where there is economic demand.

And economic demand is not the same as economic need.

There are billions of people who need the great inventions

of the computer age, and many more basic needs as well. But they have no way of expressing their needs in ways that matter to markets. So they go without.

If we are going to have a serious chance of changing their lives, we will need another level of innovation. Not just technology innovation—we need system innovation. That's what I want to discuss with you here in Davos today.

Let me begin by expressing a view that might not be widely shared.

The world is getting better.

In significant and far-reaching ways, the world is a better place to live than it has ever been.

Consider the status of women and minorities in society—virtually any society—compared to any time in the past.

Consider that life expectancy has nearly doubled in the past one hundred years.

Consider governance—the number of people today who vote in elections, express their views, and enjoy economic freedom compared to any time in the past.

In these crucial areas, the world is getting better.

These improvements have been matched, and in some cases triggered, by advances in science, technology, and medicine. They have brought us to a high point in human welfare. We are at the start of a technology-driven revolution in what people will be able to do for one another. In the coming decades, we will have astonishing new abilities to diagnose illness, heal disease, educate the world's children, create opportunities for the poor, and harness the world's brightest minds to solve our most difficult problems.

This is how I see the world, and it should make one thing clear: I am an optimist.

But I am an impatient optimist.

The world is getting better, but it's not getting better fast enough, and it's not getting better for everyone.

The great advances in the world have often aggravated the inequities in the world. The least needy see the most improvement, and the most needy see the least—in particular the billion people who live on less than a dollar a day.

There are roughly a billion people in the world who don't get enough food, who don't have clean drinking water, who don't have electricity—the things that we take for granted.

Diseases like malaria that kill over a million people a year get far less attention than drugs to help with baldness.

Not only do these people miss the benefits of the global economy—they will suffer from the negative effects of economic growth they missed out on. Climate change will have the biggest effect on people who have done the least to cause it.

Why do people benefit in inverse proportion to their need?

Market incentives make that happen.

In a system of pure capitalism, as people's wealth rises, the financial incentive to serve them rises. As their wealth falls, the financial incentive to serve them falls—until it becomes zero. We have to find a way to make the aspects of capitalism that serve wealthier people serve poorer people as well.

The genius of capitalism lies in its ability to make self-interest serve the wider interest. The potential of a big financial return for innovation unleashes a broad set of talented people in pursuit of many different discoveries. This system driven by self-interest is responsible for the great innovations that have improved the lives of billions.

But to harness this power so it benefits everyone, we need to refine the system.

As I see it, there are two great forces of human nature: self-interest, and caring for others. Capitalism harnesses self-interest in helpful and sustainable ways, but only on behalf of those who can pay. Philanthropy and government aid channel our caring for those who can't pay, but the resources run out before they meet the need. But to provide rapid improvement for the poor, we need a system that draws in innovators and businesses in a far better way than we do today.

Such a system would have a twin mission: making profits and also improving lives for those who don't fully benefit from market forces. To make the system sustainable, we need to use profit incentives whenever we can.

At the same time, profits are not always possible when business tries to serve the very poor. In such cases, there needs to be another market-based incentive—and that incentive is recognition. Recognition enhances a company's reputation and appeals to customers; above all, it attracts good people to the organization. As such, recognition triggers a market-based reward for good behavior. In markets where profits are not possible, recognition is a proxy; where profits are possible, recognition is an added incentive.

The challenge is to design a system where market incentives, including profits and recognition, drive the change.

I like to call this new system creative capitalism—an approach where governments, businesses, and nonprofits work together to stretch the reach of market forces so that more people can make a profit, or gain recognition, doing work that eases the world's inequities.

Some people might object to this kind of "market-based social change"—arguing that if we combine sentiment with self-interest, we will not expand the reach of the market but reduce it. Yet Adam Smith—the father of capitalism and the author of *Wealth of Nations,* who believed strongly in the value of self-interest for society—opened his first book with the following lines:

"How selfish soever man may be supposed, there are evidently some principles in his nature, which interest him in the fortunes of others, and render their happiness necessary to him, though he derives nothing from it, except the pleasure of seeing it."

Creative capitalism takes this interest in the fortunes of others and ties it to our interest in our own fortunes—in ways that help advance both. This hybrid engine of self-interest and concern for others serves a much wider circle of people than can be reached by self-interest or caring alone.

My thinking on this subject has been influenced by many different experiences, including our work at Microsoft to address inequity.

For the past twenty years, Microsoft has used corporate philanthropy as a way to bring technology to people who don't have access. We've donated more than $3 billion in cash and software to try to bridge the digital divide, and that will continue.

But our greatest impact is not just free or inexpensive software by itself, but rather when we show how to use technology to create solutions. And we're committed to bring more of that expertise to the table. Our product and business groups throughout the world, and some of our very best minds at our research lab in India, are working on new products, technologies, and business models that can make computing more accessible and more affordable. In one case, we're developing a text-free interface that will enable illiterate or semiliterate people to use a PC instantly, with minimal training or assistance. In another, we're looking at how wireless technology, together with software, can avoid the expensive connectivity costs that stand in the way of computing access in rural areas. We're thinking in a much more focused way about the problems that the poorest people face, and giving our most innovative thinkers the time and resources to come up with solutions.

This kind of creative capitalism matches business expertise with needs in the developing world to find markets that are already there but are untapped. Sometimes market forces fail to make an impact in developing countries not because there's no demand, or because money is lacking, but because we don't spend enough time studying the needs and limits of that market.

This point was made eloquently in C. K. Prahalad's book *The Fortune at the Bottom of the Pyramid*, and that's had a huge influence on companies in terms of stretching the profit motive through special innovation.

When the World Health Organization tried to expand vaccination for meningitis in Africa, it didn't go straight to a vaccine manufacturer. It first went to Africa to learn what people could pay. They found out that if they wanted mothers to get this vaccine for their babies, it had to be priced under fifty cents a dose. Then they challenged the partners to meet this price, and, in fact, Serum Institute in India found a new way to make the vaccine for forty cents each. The company agreed to supply 250 million doses to distribute through public health systems over the next decade, and they are free to sell it directly to the private sector too.

In another case, a Dutch company, which holds the rights to a cholera vaccine, retains the rights in the developed world but shares those rights with manufacturers in developing countries. The result is a cholera vaccine made in Vietnam that costs less than one dollar a dose—and that includes delivery and the costs of an immunization campaign. There are a number of industries that can take advantage of this kind of tiered pricing to offer valuable medicine and technology to low-income people.

These projects are just a hint of what we could accomplish if people who are experts on the needs in the developing world would meet several times a year with scientists at software or drug companies and help them try to find poor-world applications for their best ideas.

Another approach to creative capitalism includes a direct role for governments. Of course, governments do a great deal to help the poor in ways that go far beyond nurturing markets: they fund research, subsidize health care, build schools and hospitals. But some of the highest-leverage work that government can do is to set policy and disburse funds in ways that create market incentives for business activity that improves the lives of the poor.

Under a law signed by President George W. Bush last year [2007], any drug company that develops a new treatment for a neglected disease like malaria or TB can get priority review from the Food and Drug Administration for another product they've made. If you develop a new drug for malaria, your profitable cholesterol-lowering drug could go on the market a year earlier. This priority review could be worth hundreds of millions of dollars.

Another approach to creative capitalism is simply to help businesses in the poor world reach markets in the rich world. Tomorrow morning I will announce a partnership that gives African farmers access to the premium coffee market, with the goal of doubling their income from their coffee crops. This project will help African farmers produce high-quality coffee and connect them to companies that want to buy it. That will help lift them, their families, and their communities out of poverty.

Finally, one of the most inventive forms of creative capitalism involves someone we all know very well.

A few years ago, I was sitting in a bar here in Davos with Bono. After Asia and most of Europe and Africa had gone to bed, he was on fire, talking about how we could get a percentage of each purchase from civic-minded companies to help change the world. He kept calling people, waking them up, and handing me the phone. His projections were a little enthusiastic at first—but his principle was right. If you give people a chance to associate themselves with a cause they care about, they will pay more, and that premium can make an impact. That was how the RED campaign was born, here in Davos.

RED products are available from companies like Gap, Motorola, and Armani. Just this week, Dell and Microsoft joined the cause. Over the last year and a half, RED has generated $50 million for the Global Fund to Fight AIDS, TB, and Malaria. As a result, nearly two million people in Africa are receiving life-saving drugs today.

What unifies all forms of creative capitalism is that they're market-driven efforts to bring solutions we take for granted to people who can't get them. As we refine and improve this approach, there is every reason to believe these engines of change will become larger, stronger, and more efficient.

There is a growing understanding around the world that when change is driven by market-based incentives, you have a sustainable plan for change—because profits and recognition are renewable resources. Klaus Schwab runs a foundation that assists social entrepreneurs around the world, men and women who turn their ideas for improving lives into affordable goods or services. President Clinton demonstrates the unique role that a nonprofit can play as a deal maker between rich-world producers and poor-world consumers. The magazine *Fast Company* gives awards for what they call Social Capitalism.

These are not a few isolated stories; this is a worldwide movement, and we all have the ability and the responsibility to accelerate it.

I'd like to ask everyone here—whether you're in business, government, or the nonprofit world—to take on a project of creative capitalism in the coming year. It doesn't have to be a new project; you could take an existing project, and see where you might stretch the reach of market forces to help push things forward. When you award foreign aid, when you make charitable gifts, when you try to change the world—can you also find ways to put the power of market forces behind the effort to help the poor?

I hope corporations will consider dedicating a percentage of your top innovators' time to issues that could help people left out of the global economy. This kind of contribution is much more powerful than simply giving away cash or offering your employees time off to volunteer. It is a focused use of what your company does best. It is a great form of creative capitalism, because it takes the brainpower that makes life better for the richest and dedicates it to improving the lives of everyone else.

There are a number of pharmaceutical companies—Glaxo-SmithKline in particular—that are putting their top innovators to work on new approaches to help the poor. Other companies are doing the same—in food, technology, cell phones. If we could take the leaders in these areas as models, and get the rest to match them, we could make a dramatic impact against the world's inequities.

Finally, I hope that the great thinkers here will dedicate some time to finding ways for businesses, governments, NGOs, and the media to create measures of what companies are doing to use their power and intelligence to serve a wider circle of people. This kind of information is an important element of creative capitalism. It can turn good works into recognition, and ensure that recognition brings market-based rewards to businesses that do the most work to serve the most people.

We are living in a phenomenal age. If we can spend the early decades of the twenty-first century finding approaches that meet the needs of the poor in ways that generate profits and recognition for business, we will have found a sustainable way to reduce poverty in the world. This task is open-ended. It can never be finished. But a passionate effort to answer this challenge will help change the world.

CREATIVE CAPITALISM: THE CHEAT SHEET

Michael Kinsley

This is my attempt to summarize Bill's speech. In academia, this is known as a "cheat sheet." In the business world, it is called an "executive summary."

1. Today's miracles of technology benefit only those who can afford them. Markets respond only to "demand," not to "need."

2. This is a systemic flaw in the free-market system. Further technological innovation is less important than systemic innovation to mend this flaw.

3. The world is getting better, but not fast enough and not for everyone. Great advances in technology therefore make inequity worse. About a billion people are left out. For example, climate change will impose the worst effects on those least responsible for it.

4. Why? Because in "a system of pure capitalism," the incentive to serve people rises as their wealth rises and falls as their wealth falls. This system needs to be changed so that there is incentive to serve poor people too.

5. Self-interest is just one of two forces in human nature. The other is "caring for others." The genius of capitalism is that it makes self-interest serve the general interest. Philanthropy and government are supposed to address our "caring for others," but there isn't enough philanthropic or government money to solve the world's problems.

6. A revised capitalist system would both make a profit and improve the lives of the have-nots.

7. A revised system should use profit incentives where possible. But even where profits are not possible, there is a market-based incentive that can be used: recognition. Positive recognition is good for a company's reputation, good for attracting customers, and good for attracting employees.

8. Creative capitalism is a system where incentives for both profit and recognition motivate both self-interest and caring for others.

9. Under creative capitalism governments, businesses, and non-profits work together.

10. "This hybrid engine of self-interest and concern for others serves a much wider circle of people than can be reached by self-interest or caring alone."

11. Example: Corporations donating money or products. Or, even better, corporations spending money or using technology to find new markets in poor countries.

12. Example: "tiered pricing." A drug company has a valuable patent and charges full monopoly price in the developed world, but lets poor-world manufacturers produce for less than one dollar a dose.

13. Sometimes there is a "direct role for government": creating market incentives for companies to help the poor. For example, the FDA rules that if you develop a new treatment for a neglected disease, you get priority review by the FDA for some other drug.

14. Another approach: Help poor-world businesses do business in developed world.

15. Another example: the Bono ("RED" campaign) model. Sell products with a small percentage of the profits going to worthy causes in the poor world. People will pay more for products associated with these causes.

16. "What unifies all forms of creative capitalism is that they are market-driven efforts to bring solutions we take for granted to people who can't get them."

17. Corporations should allow "top innovators" to spend part of their time on issues facing people too poor to be customers. This "takes the brainpower that makes life better for the richest, and dedicates it to improving the lives of everyone else."

BILL GATES AND WARREN BUFFETT DISCUSS "CREATIVE CAPITALISM"

Warren Buffett and Bill Gates

This is the edited transcript of a discussion between Bill Gates and Warren Buffett about Bill's concept of creative capitalism. The discussion, over lunch at the Gates residence in Medina, Washington, took place on May 15, 2008. Also at the table were Melinda Gates, Josh Daniel of the Gates Foundation, and me. I started by asking Warren what he thought of the whole idea

—Michael Kinsley

WARREN BUFFETT: I would rather have Bill, if he will, give me the main points.

BILL GATES: Well, it's not completely well defined. I totally believe in markets as such powerful forces for drawing out innovation. And yet you do get trapped in this situation where the markets serve where the dollars are, so you don't get markets meeting the needs of the poorest. And so how do you bootstrap or support the needs of the poorest so markets are reaching out to them? I mean, when I view the last hundred years as an experiment in how good markets are, the answer is very, very clear and very strong. It's one of those things that's so clear people won't even discuss it with you anymore. Like in this [Edward] Teller book: he says, Look, if he didn't believe in innovation, he would have been a communist. If the economy is a zero-sum situation, then you ought to try some crazy sharing thing. It's only the innovation and pie-growing activity that made Teller feel comfortable with the capitalistic approach. And I think that that's been validated.

You often hear people saying that companies should do something besides profit maximization. And it's amazing how strong a message is hidden in words like "diversity" or the broad term "corporate social responsibility." Warren and I were just at the Microsoft CEO Summit for the last couple days, and it was amazing how many of the talks were about how a company needs to have core values of who they are and what they do as the thing that makes the employees feel they have a purpose and guides their action. And how that needs to be really at the center, even more so than the short-term profit metrics. Jack Welch was very good on that and Lee Scott [CEO of Wal-Mart] was very good on that, I think in a very sincere way. I think it's more true all the time.

Bill George [of Harvard Business School] ran the leadership panel, and he was saying how the younger generation really wants to go to work with people who have a purpose. So what I'm saying is when people write down that purpose, when they write down their values, that an element of that should be: What can we do based on our skill set, our innovators, whatever unique capacities we have as a company — what can we be doing for the poorest two billion? And that can either be taking more risk in terms of trying to develop markets there, which is C.K. Prahalad–type stuff, or just doing things that are not profit seeking and yet not giving up a huge percentage of profit.

So somebody can read the words "creative capitalism" and say, "Okay, Bill Gates said that you should serve the poorest two billion and ignore profit." That is not what I intend to say at all, but then I am being a bit ambiguous about how far you go in being willing to give up something. Am I saying one percent? Two percent? Three percent? Nobody who sets these dual roles is very good about being clear. I mean, what do they say you're supposed to give up for corporate social responsibility? Well, they're not willing to be numeric, because they feel like the two goals—profit and social responsibility—aren't totally at odds over time.

I understand it best in terms of the big companies of the world: pharma, banks, technology companies, food companies. Buying from the poor world, supplying to the poor world, having scientists and innovators who come together to think about the poor world. It's best defined for me there, and then I think, "Okay, how concrete is this?" I go back to this thing of: Okay, if all companies did as well as the best do, then it would be pretty dramatic in terms of the rate of improvement for the poorest. And a year from now, I'll know a lot more about this, because in my new time back at the foundation I'll meet with heads of pharma, heads of food companies, heads of . . . I'll meet a lot of these companies and try and get a sense of, do they agree that in their hiring it would help them, do they agree that in their reputation and maybe seeking long-term markets it would help them and see how concrete a response is possible.

WARREN: But as Bill was talking, it just occurred to me that if you don't trust the government to do a lot of things very well—and business will never trust them to do that; rich people will never trust them to do that—and if, on the other hand, the honor system doesn't work particularly well in terms of how many people behave—and this idea just occurred to me ten seconds ago, so it will take a lot of refining. What if you had three percent or something like that of the corporate income tax totally devoted to a fund that would be administered by some representatives of corporate America to be used in intelligent ways for the long-term benefit of society? This group—who think they can run things way better than government—could tackle education, health, et cetera, or other activities in which government has a large role. And it would have this forced funding of three percent of corporate profits or some sum like that. Ace Greenberg used to insist that all the managing directors of Bear Stearns give four percent to charity, and in December of each year he would go around and talk to everyone who hadn't yet given his four percent. And he told all the Jews that they had to give any shortfall at year-end to Catholic Charities, and he told the Catholics they had to give it to the United Jewish Appeal. Well, this would be a variation on that. Take three percent—pick a figure—of corporate income. That would be, perhaps, $30 billion a year; you would exempt small companies. If there are things to be done in society that the market system doesn't naturally lead to, something like this would be a supplement to the invisible hand. It would be a second hand that would come down for society—administered in a businesslike manner—and it might be interesting to see what a system like that might produce.

BILL: You might want to say that companies could include the cost of putting their best innovators on to the problems, and say that if you don't do that, then you have to pay it out in cash, and it goes into a pool for the businesses that do have the innovators and might want to devote four percent or five percent. When we go to a drug company and say, "Work on a malaria vaccine," it's completely unreasonable to expect them to fund it themselves. And so you do get this weird thing—I don't know how much I've said this in speeches; I think I've said it privately more—where it's better for a large drug company to say, "We don't work on the diseases for the poor. But if we did, we'd give it away." And then you have these other drug companies that do work on diseases for the poor [and] they actually get discredit because they're charging their marginal cost, where the other guy could pontificate and say, "Yeah, we don't happen to have any, but boy, we wouldn't be like those bastards and charge for the thing."

WARREN: The market system is always going to take care of the medical needs of the rich. If a rich guy wants to take out a young gal, you're going to sell him Viagra and be able to make money doing so. Basically, the market system will make that research worthwhile. But it won't make research worthwhile for some disease that is indigenous to the poorest parts of the world and not present elsewhere.

MIKE: Two of the biggest categories of creative capitalism seem to be, first, one way or another, a corporation gives away money or money equivalents like the time of its best employees, and second, corporations seeking out profit-making opportunities in poorer countries that they otherwise might not. Let me ask you about the second one. It's sort of like the famous joke about the economist who sees the ten-dollar bill on the ground and says it can't be there, someone would have picked it up. Why does it require creative capitalism to . . . I mean, if there is great opportunity there, why aren't people doing it already?

WARREN: Market opportunities will be filled. I think the present system works pretty well in terms of real market opportunities. Now, there are a lot of people who would like things to be market opportunities that aren't market opportunities. But I don't worry very much about real market opportunities not getting filled.

BILL: You definitely want to encourage people to go into countries where it would be normally riskier and they might not choose to go. A country like Vietnam is improving its situation without much help from creative capitalism. They've gotten governance basically right, the education thing is right, they're getting population growth at a level where they can really feed and employ their people. It's a spectacular thing. In an earlier question, we talked about which are the most important elements. Government plus normal capitalism—really good government plus normal capitalism. If you can have that, God bless you, that is such a fantastic thing. It works very well.

But when you get this problem of these diseases—this sounds like an awful thing to say—but when diseases affect both rich and poor countries, trickle-down will eventually work for the poorest, because the high cost of development is recovered in the rich world and then, as they go off patent, they're sold for marginal cost to the poor, and everybody benefits. But the fact that malaria was eliminated in the United States and we don't need a malaria vaccine is a tiny bit of a tragedy, because you don't have all of these brilliant minds at work to solve this problem. This is where you need creative capitalism. Like getting micronutrients to the poor, getting these drug discovery things done. Trying to use the cell phone and network in a different way. The rich world can fall into a way of doing something that works for them that doesn't work for the poor world.

WARREN: The market also gets distorted where you feel you're going to get screwed after going into a country. You're going to set a higher threshold on expected returns if you think there's a fair chance they're going to expropriate your assets. And, if there is no rule of law at all, you may skip the country regardless of possible returns.

MIKE: But that's rational.

WARREN: Yeah, absolutely rational. Now the counterbalance of that is to have something like a federal export-import bank—a bank that insures foreign purchases—that says if you go to, say, Indonesia and they take your assets away from you, well, at least they guarantee you will get your cost back. But government has a role to play in that. Otherwise, it is perfectly rational for me to say I'm not going to go back to Indonesia again because we got screwed. That will always be the case with some countries, although I think it's way less of a deterrent now than it was twenty-five years ago. Nevertheless, expropriation risk—including confiscating taxes that might later be imposed—will still deter people bringing goods and services to people in some areas of the world.

MIKE: Bill, can people or sometimes companies irrationally seek comfort and avoid risk? And if it's not irrational, why should you force people to do it?

BILL: Well, rationality only goes so far. If your young employees are saying to you, "Hey, should we be trying to develop the market in Africa?" rationality might say to you, "Gosh, we don't pay much attention to that, why bother?" There's a lot of latitude in terms of what's rational. If you feel like getting involved in that, if it has this positive benefit, then you'll put more time into the specific strategy that is rational to going after that opportunity and maybe coming up with something that in the long term is very rational.

There are multiple rational paths that companies can go down. If you said to a company, "Hey, your diversity policy made you do irrational things versus what you would have done without a diversity policy," they will say, "Oh no, it just opened our eyes to better rationality." And some of them will be telling the truth. I think a lot of them will be telling the truth. Some will just—of course, they don't really know. You don't get to live path A and path B and then subtract and say, "Okay, the one that is bigger is the rational one and the other one is kind of the stupid one."

WARREN: I would say that it may well be at Microsoft that progressive policies make some difference in terms of whom they are able to hire. But I think if you took Kraft versus Kellogg versus General Mills—and General Mills happens to be in Minneapolis, where they have that 5 percent corporate donation program—I don't think it has any real effect on the quality of who applies for jobs at the three companies. You take GEICO. If GEICO has a policy of being green, or whatever, when we are recruiting, I don't think it makes much difference to prospective employees.

MIKE: So let's talk about situations where creative capitalism is frankly going to cost you something and it's like you're reducing the return to shareholders. And question one is, Why do corporate managers have the right to do that?

WARREN: I don't think they do. Basically, I don't feel I've got the right to give away shareholders' money, though I feel our shareholders should have the right to designate part of their share of profits to go to their own charitable priorities. I mean, I may believe in women's reproductive rights or something like that, and if I want to give all my personal money to that, that's fine. But I don't think other shareholders should have to support my preferences. However, I think it would be nice if we had a mechanism whereby the people who favored adoption would be able to devote their proportional share of Berkshire's charitable funds to that purpose, and so on.

MIKE: I thought you had a program like that.

WARREN: We did for twenty or twenty-five years, but we had people who objected to some of the places the money was going, and they were putting so much heat—not on us or on our employees, but on suppliers and others who work with us—and I just wasn't willing to fight them on that. But I still believe that this kind of program where stockholders pick the places their money goes is the right approach. When the government bureaucrats allocate the taxpayers' money, all the rich guys get mad about it. But when the rich guys are allocating their shareholders' money, they seem to think that God gave them that right.

BILL: Let me take a case that's really clear-cut, which is the Microsoft case. We need to have great relationships with governments all over the world. And because we make a product whose marginal cost of production is very low—software—and because information empowerment is so directly what we're about, it's not a stretch in any way, the idea that we go into over one hundred countries and do these things where we donate massive amounts of software. We even give cash gifts, and we train teachers. And we make sure we get visibility for that and we make sure when we hire employees they know about that. When we're competing for government contracts, we remind people we're a good citizen in that country. I can't do the math for you in some hyper-rational way. I suppose you could go overboard on it, but versus not doing that, Microsoft is absolutely way better off.

Now, the thing we've done that I don't know if we'll get credit for it—but I love it and I think we probably will—is we have the lab in India specialize in looking out for the poorest. And it was very interesting, because when they came in to present to me, they had a few slides up front that said . . . they call it bottom of the pyramid, bottom two billion. They had a few slides up front that said PCs are too expensive, electricity is too hard, we're going to show you something here where Microsoft software actually plays a modest role. And it's this thing where they use DVDs—it's really cool—to help teachers and to help farmers. But literally it's a TV set and a portable DVD player they can use to figure out best practices, like *American Idol*. You get the local farmers together, they compete, they video the best one, and they create a social event where they take that out and play that DVD. It didn't use a lot of Microsoft software, but so what. It's a very clever idea. They're going to spin off, the people are so committed they're going to go do this full-time, and the Gates Foundation is looking at how we can support them as they plan to scale this thing up. So it's a minor part. If you did the math, I think there were thirty people in the lab who were broadly working on this stuff in a sixty-thousand-person company. Has that got some direct payoff? I bet it does.

WARREN: If I'm chairman of ExxonMobil, though, and I think that Nigeria is a particularly attractive oil province to go to work in, do I give ten million dollars to the favorite charity of the president of Nigeria, or do I poll the lower class of Nigeria to see what they'd really like done for them and spend the ten million dollars there? I mean, if you're really following market economics, you do want people to think favorably of you, but different companies may want different people feeling favorably about them, and all this may have very little to do with what society would like if you had a social equation that you were weighing. On a strictly market test, it may be better to have a dictator or his wife think well of you than take an action that benefits his millions of subjects.

MIKE: Isn't there a sort of catch-22 logic at work where you say that spending this money is justified for the shareholders because the goodwill pays off in various ways, helps you hire better people, gets you into Nigeria—

WARREN: Or keeps you out of trouble.

MIKE: Yes. But then if it really does pay off, why do you still have bragging rights? If what you're buying is bragging rights that you do good—and those have value, therefore it's justified in terms of your imposition on the shareholders—well, in that case you don't deserve the bragging rights.

BILL: Yes you do, because you've pushed the world in the right direction. There is such a thing as a win-win in this world. If you figure out how to give good customer service, you are allowed to brag about how you have great customer service. If you figure out how to make governments love you by helping the poor people in that country, you get both the benefit of the government loving you and you get to say you helped the poor in that country.

WARREN: As long as you don't say what you're doing is to get bragging rights?

BILL: No, no. Microsoft is very honest to saying that it's not purely our doing. Partners in Learning, which is the school donation thing. That's not purely . . . we don't go to the world news and say, "Oh, we're just suffering so much; this was so hard." The world is more like this. College kids do really want to associate themselves in their full-time work activity with something beyond just how profitable the institution they're involved in is. Now, maybe that's a very elite statement, maybe that's more an upper-tier, particular group of people, but if you take the big global companies, that's the hiring pool that they care the most about.

WARREN: The people at Wal-Mart would rather work for an admired company than a company where they're criticized every day. I don't think they care that much about the specific policies that lead to the criticism or admiration, but there's no question you feel better about going to work for a company that's admired or your kids feel better because they hear different things at school. But at Wal-Mart I think most employees care about the policies that will directly affect them. I'm not sure how much they really care about the other issues.

With our shareholder designation plan, we had reverse publicity. In the end some people boycotted See's Candies because of what our shareholders were giving to, even though other shareholders were giving to things that the boycotters agreed with. The boycotters picked out the things they didn't like rather than the things they did like.*

BILL: They didn't even give you the net benefit of the—

WARREN: No. We regularly pointed out that it was totally the shareholders making the decision. We had lots of money going to Catholic schools and all that. One guy wrote me and said I don't care if you give a billion dollars to pro-life organizations and a dollar to a pro-choice organization, he says, I'm still boycotting you. People feel very strongly sometimes, often in inverse relationship to the logic of their argument.

MIKE: One thing you're proud of at the Gates Foundation is the way you focus and the way you make very rational, business-like, and to the extent you can, testable decisions about where you devote your resources. What confidence do you have that this much more amorphous process you're describing here, where corporations want to have good relations with the government of Peru or want their employees in India to feel good and so on, will have anything like that kind of discipline in where the resources go?

BILL: Well, discipline is always based on feedback systems, economic or otherwise, and so corporations are very, as Warren was saying, very influenced by reputational feedback. Almost slavishly so. I mean, there are some things about how you do corporate structure that just get done without even that much evaluation because somebody who does a point system on governance has chosen that to get these points we have to do such and such. What we need is a body of industry-specific expertise

---

* For many years Berkshire Hathaway had a program whereby individual shareholders could pick charities to which the company would donate.

and someone to do an analysis on, say, a yearly basis of what this company did that is in this creative capitalism category and here's the impact that we think that's going to have. And that type of feedback system, I think, is a necessary element of keeping the score in some fair way and making sure that when these resources are used brilliantly, that the best practices are spread and when they're not, there isn't too much credit. I'll be the first to admit that it's very easy to make statements about this that sound good and only by taking a lot of time to dig into it do you find out that it had no impact at all, it wasn't that much money, it was something that we were going to do anyway. There's a lot of room for fluffery in this space, and so you've got to bring in expertise and that will probably take a while to develop.

MIKE: In Washington, I was always struck by the fact that there would be these lavish parties to celebrate, say, ExxonMobil's contribution to *Masterpiece Theatre*. And then you'd look it up and it turned out, well, they spent three dollars bragging about how wonderful they were for every dollar they spent being wonderful.

WARREN: I've been on the board of a number of places where I've watched the charitable dynamics. One was the Urban Institute. The truth is, I could walk in to the CEO of any company and get fifty thousand dollars or one hundred thousand dollars for the Urban Institute if Berkshire owned their stock or if I was on the board or Berkshire was a huge customer. The whole thing was based on figuring out who was connected to whom, and one time I brought it up . . . I said, "Do you ever list all the wonderful things the Urban Institute is doing and then ask the CEO for his own personal contribution?" They said, "Don't do that! Just ask for the corporate money." Having been on a lot of boards, a number of the boards even let the directors make certain charitable contributions and matching contributions, all that sort of thing. I think Bill, however, could actually go to Pfizer or some other company and have some real impact. He's personally contributing substantial sums, which is impressive, he's calling personally, and he knows the subject. He could have some impact. Very few people can.

BILL: I do draw a distinction between the company drawing on its natural expertise like the drug company doing a drug or a Coke company with its distribution system or Nestlé buying more food from poor farmers or helping put micronutrients in that don't make the food taste bad. I draw a big distinction between that and writing a check. If ExxonMobil employees actually did the *Masterpiece Theatre* thing or some brilliant thing about crude oil, maybe they're drawing on something unique there.

MIKE: Well, suppose I was a shareholder of Microsoft or even suppose I wasn't, but I came to you and said, "Bill, rather than trying to come up with all sorts of ways Microsoft can make the world a better place, some of which—maybe even most of which—aren't going to help the bottom line, I would much rather you do everything you can do to make Microsoft profitable and then take the money that you made and spend it directly on what you have figured out to be the most efficient way to make the world a better place."

BILL: I think that would be a mistake, because what we get in countries around the world where our employees are volunteering to train teachers in these schools, where they are taking some of the time that we pay them to train teachers in these schools, and where we're making cash donations to training— the leverage we get by donating free software and the leverage we get by having seen countries that do this well—and there are a lot of countries that are very open minded that say, "Hey, show us how to do this well." And where we can have them go visit the other country and see it. They are really interested in what those pitfalls are going to be, and, you know, the world's not just about money. It's about expertise. The developing world has a huge shortage of expertise, and to that degree Microsoft, either from its rich-world employees or spreading best practices from one developing country to the next, has a huge impact, though it's hard to measure. The amount of money we—say we canceled all this stuff, it wouldn't be more than two to three percent of what we do. In some of the poorer countries, it would be twenty percent of what Microsoft does, but not that high.

MIKE: And you feel you've got a twenty percent payoff even there?

BILL: Well, in those countries, it's when we're first establishing our business and our business is quite small, and the early relationship with the government is the main thing. Take Indonesia, where I just was. We're down to where maybe ten percent of what we do is not direct profit seeking but helping education, helping with community centers. It's about ten percent. And that's not counting the value of the donated software. If you count the value of the donated software, you can get some big number, but that's a fanciful number in the sense that it's not business forgone. There was not a path where those dollars came into our sales number.

WARREN: I think corporations, though, much like many foundations, will focus locally. That's the natural tendency. If you take that Minneapolis group, you know, it started many decades ago and you really pledged, if you were a major corporation, that you were going to spend a significant portion of profits on philanthropy. Target is 5 percent, I think.

BILL: Five percent?

WARREN: Yeah, 5 percent.

BILL: Five percent of their profits goes to—

WARREN: Yeah.

BILL: That's amazing.

MIKE: There's a third category of creative capitalism, which is like the RED campaign. Basically, consumers will apparently pay a premium for a product if they know that part of it is going to go to charity. I would ask Warren: isn't that a little irrational?

WARREN: Yeah. I don't think it works that well. If you have a specific cause for a short time—there's a local tornado in Omaha or a tsunami far away—it's both humane and politically correct to respond. I don't think it's something that sustains itself over time. I don't think that if we announced at GEICO, you know, 2 percent of your premiums were going to help people around the world, only a few would want to pay an extra 2 percent. The rest would say, reduce my premium and give it to me.

BILL: I agree with that in terms of car insurance. When people buy clothing, you know, my daughter's not saying, you know,

"Do these Juicy sweatpants wear out in n years and have a certain stiffness?" or things like that. She's associating herself to the degree we fund her to do so with Juicy. And so the RED question—which I admit is out, but I think it's a great experiment and I'm somewhat optimistic—is can you create a brand association for consumers in the U.S. if there are some products like their credit card, their clothing, their cell phone? And you have to be very creative in coming up with new things and keeping those fresh. Is there a brand association with RED products that you feel proud that you've done that and it's kind of a cool thing? That's where branding people are needed to help us achieve, and I think and I hope the answer is yes. I'm not saying that all products in the economy should all go off and have some, you know, bleeding-heart two percent payoff thing. I'm not saying that at all.

Even if it is grandly successful, this will be a tiny part of the economy. It's not going to generate billions of dollars. But it is also a nice vehicle for us to raise awareness of these causes and ideally activate people to either volunteer or vote in a way that is beneficial to these causes as well.

WARREN: There are twenty other variables, but Gap's in-store sales are falling month by month. There are a lot of other variables. Believe me, they were falling before, but it is . . . I think it's tough to build a sustainable thing. I'm not saying it's impossible, but I don't yet see the evidence.

MIKE: Is it ever going to work on you as a consumer?

WARREN: Never has.

BILL: Well, Warren's not much of a consumer.

WARREN: In fact, I'm not much of a consumer at all.

BILL: Think about how you're brand conscious in something you buy. When you buy golf balls, what do you think? You buy a brand.

WARREN: You buy a brand. You're buying what you hope is distance. You do.

MICHAEL: So how much distance would you give up for part of the cost of your golf balls to go to AIDS?

WARREN: The difference is a matter of a yard or two. I'm not giving up anything important.

BILL: If brands . . . brands are about an association, and it's not irrational that there could be a brand that was about being associated with helping with AIDS. It's a new pioneering thing that . . . it's done pretty well so far.

MIKE: I just want to take another crack at something. Suppose you were running the world. Would there be a place for creative capitalism like this in it? Or would it be much more rational? Would you say, "Look, corporations should be efficient and produce products and then we should decide what we wish to achieve as a society and we all pay taxes and do it."

WARREN: I would have my own tax system, but the answer is I think I would go the second route.

BILL: I think there are going to be corporations that will build problem-solving expertise that does not exist anyplace else. And your hypothetical is a little strange because what we're faced with is a world with vast disparities in wealth that have to do with what country you're born into, and you wouldn't have that if you had one person running the world, and so, you know, the degree to which a little bit of innovation can make a huge, huge difference—whether it's an LED flashlight or something you can roll to move the water that you used to have to carry.

Some of these innovations—when you see them you say, "Oh, well, obviously that rationally should have happened," but it only happened because somebody cared. Now, you could say in the grand sweep of time capitalistic economics would have come up with that. Well, there's a lot of suffering between now and eventually that this thing can deal with.

CREATIVE CAPITALISM: A STARTING CRITIQUE

Michael Kinsley

When I asked Greg Mankiw, former chief economic adviser to the second President Bush, to join this discussion of "creative capitalism," he said, "I thought capitalism *was* creative." So problem number one may be linguistic. The term "creative capitalism" was coined, or at least popularized, by the most successful capitalist in the history of the world. But in a way it's an insult to capitalism just as George W. Bush's legendary "compassionate conservatism" is an insult to other conservatives. If George Bush is a "compassionate conservative," what are all the other conservatives? If there is something called "creative" capitalism, does that mean that ordinary capitalism isn't creative?

Obviously, Bill Gates does not mean that. But he obviously does mean to say that capitalism can be improved upon. And specifically, a new, improved capitalism could address some problems that neither today's capitalism nor philanthropy nor government is dealing with adequately. He sees capitalism as potentially superior to the other two because it is limitless—or at least our own capitalist system is far bigger than either the government or the philanthropic sector. And neither of these, he says, is big enough to do the job.

But is creative capitalism actually a new kind of capitalism? Or is it just a grab bag of proposals that bear some relationship to the theory of free markets? Consider, for example, school choice, vouchers, charter schools, and so forth. These policies try to use market forces as a way to make schools better. But the basic principle involved is more socialist than capitalist: that society has an obligation to provide a decent public primary and secondary education to everyone, whether they can afford it or not.

Capitalism as a "system" isn't a set of rules that was enacted once upon a time and now can be easily amended. It is an arrangement that has grown organically from roots deep in human nature. Truly amending it would be more than just a matter of changing the rules.

So one big question raised by Bill's speech is whether we are talking about an actual change in the nature of capitalism or just about a series of techniques that require noncapitalist motivations to work. In other words, Bill says he wants to move beyond government and philanthropy and use capitalism itself to solve the world's problems. But most of his specific ideas are at bottom philanthropic, and they ultimately depend on the generous instincts of rich people, which are not bottomless, or on government, which means the generous instincts of the voters, which are not bottomless either.

Selfishness is so built into the concept of free-market capitalism that the idea of making a role for selflessness seems nearly hopeless. For that reason, the most interesting and original notion in Bill's speech was the concept of "recognition" as something that can be a substitute for self-interest as a capitalist incentive. Recognition is a possible answer to those who say that the purpose of capitalism is profit maximization. But there is some ambiguity in this concept of recognition as Bill describes it. Is recognition an actual alternative to self-interest or simply another route to getting there? In other words, is the idea that companies should devote some fraction of their profits to good works because the shareholders crave recognition, or is it because being recognized as a company that does good works will lead people to buy more of the company's product, will make it easier to hire top-notch employees, and so on, leading to a payoff to shareholders of the traditional sort?

In either case, other questions arise. If the hunger for recognition is a natural force inside all of us that is similar to self-interest of the traditional sort, where has it been for the past few centuries? And why do we now have to amend the capitalist system in order to exploit this force? This is, I suppose, just a version of the old joke about the rational-expectations economist who doesn't pick up a ten-dollar bill he sees on the sidewalk because if it were really there someone would have picked it up already. If recognition can be such a powerful force, why isn't it a powerful force already?

If, on the other hand, recognition is just a branding strategy—companies can profit from a reputation for valuing other things besides profits—we are in the world of the catch-22. Companies spend their stockholders' money in ways other than maximizing profits for the shareholders because a reputation for not maximizing profits is the best way to maximize profits. And yet if they are actually maximizing profits, then the recognition for not maximizing profits is undeserved and is basically a con.

Before there was creative capitalism, there was "corporate responsibility." This came in two flavors. The right-wing version was also called "shareholders' rights" and was the ideological justification for the corporate raiders and leveraged buyouts of the 1980s. They argued that corporate management was pursuing its own interests and not those of the shareholders. (This was the same argument made years earlier by the left-wing economist John Kenneth Galbraith, to no acclaim in the business world.) The left-wing version of corporate responsibility was an argument that corporations had responsibilities beyond those to its shareholders. This is where the concept of "stakeholders" came from: a group that included employees, members of the communities where the company was located, and ultimately all those affected by the company's behavior. The notion that a company owed good behavior (however defined) to all these people was a close predecessor of creative capitalism, which assumes that companies have a responsibility of some sort to everyone on the planet.

But where does this responsibility come from? Why isn't it best if corporations concentrate on maximizing profits, allowing capitalism to perform its alchemy of turning profit maximization (aka "greed") into social good and allowing government and voluntary private charities to fill in the gaps? Bill's answer is that the gaps are too big—more like chasms. The problems are too formidable for governments and private charities to handle. Only the private capitalist economy is big enough to handle it. But this doesn't really explain why the private economy should tackle these problems. "Recognition" is a good crack at an answer, because it fits right into the familiar mechanisms of capitalism.

In his speech, Bill offers five reasonably specific examples of creative capitalism in action, each of which raises some questions.

1. *Simple corporate philanthropy: corporations giving away goods or cash to people who desperately need it.* The main objection to this is that corporate managers have no right to be giving away the shareholders' money. Free-market purists would say that this denies individuals the freedom to spend their own money as they wish. And anyway, much of the payoff in "recognition" goes to the corporate managers—Medicis and Rockefellers with other people's money—rather than to the stockholders. The answer to that complaint is that if the corporate policy is clear, people who object don't have to buy the stock in the first place. But is there a better answer?

2. *Corporations should look harder for existing but underserved markets in poor countries.* Or, a bit farther down the road, corporations should look harder for ways in which firms in poor countries can market their products in advanced countries. In other words, there is profitable business to be done—profitable in the traditional, noncreative capitalist sense—that is not done because "we don't spent enough time studying the needs and limits," as Bill says. The question is, Why not? There is profitable business just sitting there, but nobody picks it up because of . . . what? Racism? Lazy thinking? Protectionism? If so, this is truly the low-hanging fruit of creative capitalism and it's hard to imagine anyone objecting to it. The objection would have to be that it can't be this easy or someone would have done it already. (That ten-dollar bill again.) Or maybe that finding and developing these markets is disproportionately expensive and can't be justified on a straight traditional-capitalist basis even if the effort would ultimately pay off. In that case, we're back at example one, asking what justifies using the shareholders' money to pursue charity.

3. *"Tiered pricing."* That is, selling your product (typically, pharmaceuticals) for one price in the developed world and a much lower price in poor countries. It is easier to justify this for some products than for others. Products of the "new economy"— pharmaceuticals, software, and so on—are generally very expensive to develop and very cheap to produce. It may cost a billion dollars to get to the first pill and a penny to produce the second, the third, and so on. Pricing these products rationally is difficult to impossible. If you charge the marginal cost, as we are taught in Econ 101, you will never recover your development expenses. If you set a price that will enable you to recover those expenses, you will be leaving piles of money on the table (from people who could afford to pay more than the marginal cost of production but not the higher price reflecting the cost of development). You also will be denying the benefit of your drug to people who need it desperately.

"Tiered pricing" is a genteel name for price discrimination, which is frowned upon ordinarily. In theory, it's even impossible in a competitive market, where no seller can charge more than the marginal cost. And even in practice, there is leakage: When you cross the border from Canada to the United States these days, the customs officials are looking for prescription drugs as much as recreational ones.

If companies are supposed to charge less for traditional products—which presumably are already sold at something close to marginal cost—we run into the same question that came up in example one: What is the justification for using the stockholders' money in this way? And what is so "creative" (or, for that matter, "capitalist") about it? Isn't it just charity?

4. *The government creates market incentives for companies to help poor people and poor nations.* Example: for every drug a pharmaceutical company develops to treat some neglected disease of the poor, the FDA gives the company expedited approval for some other drug of their choice.

This one is really problematic. Why does drug number two need expedited review? Is it because there is a logjam of new drugs waiting for FDA approval? Then surely the answer is either: (a) triage the waiting list and give "expedited" slots to the drugs that promise to do the most good, not ones that happen to be made by companies with neglected drugs awaiting approval; or (b) expand the resources of the FDA so that people can reap the benefit of newly developed drugs as soon as possible. Or, if the problem is that the FDA drug-approval process is overly cautious and risk-averse, it seems nuts to start making unrelated exemptions to that process rather than reforming it. And if there is nothing in particular wrong with the normal FDA review process, granting "expedited" review must mean lowering safety standards. One way or another, this example seems like government using its own incompetence as a weapon for blackmail.

5. *The Bono model:* charge people a premium for the recognition value of products associated with worthy causes (such as Bono's RED campaign), and use the money for projects that help the world's poor. In the bad old days of antitrust, this would have been called a "tying arrangement"—forcing you to buy one product in order to buy another—and was thought to promote monopoly. That notion is pretty well discredited now. Still, questions arise. In particular: How much is being spent on advertising and promotion in order to create the recognition value that is being sold to customers? How much is being spent on administration of the campaign? How much is being spent on self-congratulation by the executives of the participating companies? When you net all that out, how much is left for the programs to help the world's poor? And what kind of supervision and discipline is there to make sure that the money is well spent?

The basic question for creative capitalism is: Why shouldn't the entire capitalist system do what Bill did, rather than what he now advocates? That is, why shouldn't capitalism go about its business: enriching some people, benefiting many more by transforming greed into social gain, and creating wealth that can be, and often will be, given away?

One answer to that could be to bring us back to the ten-dollar-bill problem. Maybe the bill was actually there. Capitalism does evolve. People do make new discoveries, and not all of them are technological or medical. It's not at all impossible that, for example, the potential power of recognition as a motivator in the free-market system is waiting to be exploited simply because no one ever thought of it before. Isn't it?

THE CASE FOR CREATIVE CAPITALISM

Ed Glaeser

The fact that private businesspeople are leading the charge against worldwide misery is the result of two great failures. First, Mr. Gates's speech reminds us that while laissez-faire capitalism has worked many miracles, it never has been particularly well targeted toward righting social inequities. Private firms usually have better incentives to cater to the rich than to the poor. The labor market rewards those with skills, not the illiterate and innumerate. Perhaps in the long run, an unfettered private education sector might spread human capital worldwide, but it would surely take centuries before the children of Africa received the same quality education as their counterparts in Sweden.

The case for creative capitalism is based as much on a second failure—the failure of government. After all, most governments have explicitly taken on the responsibility for education and health care. In much of the world, they have failed dismally in that responsibility. The dismal economic performance of sub-Saharan Africa owes far more to kleptocracy and state-led violence than to anything produced by globalization.

Large sums of development aid often go missing on their journey from the pockets of first-world taxpayers to the schools and clinics of the third world. Even the generally capable and well-meaning governments of the U.S. and Europe lack the ingenuity and incentives to solve the most difficult problems.

So I am excited about the promise of creative capitalism because private social entrepreneurs have at least some chance of making up for the limitations of the public sector, especially in the developing world. To be most effective, however, creative capitalists need to tailor their intervention around the capability of the public sector. In the places of great prosperity, where the state functions well, creative capitalists can add the most by harnessing the innovative nature of the decentralized private sector. The National Institutes of Health is one of the most effective of all government programs, but private philanthropy still has plenty of new medical ideas to contribute. This is because creative capitalists can take risks that are out of reach for a government bureaucracy that is appropriately bound by rules meant to limit the waste of taxpayer dollars.

In areas where the government is weaker, creative capitalists can be most effective by filling in for the missing state. In this regard, Herbert Hoover is one of history's most effective philanthropists. During World War I, the wealthy engineer adopted the cause of feeding a starving Belgium. After the war, he led a relief effort that fed ten million people in the Soviet Union. Hoover's efforts were hardly government-free—they relied on U.S. congressional largesse—but he insisted on direct administration of relief, without the interference of Lenin's revolutionary government. Hoover's American Relief Administration became a substitute for failed government.

Many of the finest moments in philanthropy feature creative

capitalists stepping in to address similar governmental failures. By the start of the twentieth century, many local governments in America had effectively led a public health battle to provide clean water. Unsurprisingly, the Jim Crow South lagged behind. So John D. Rockefeller used his resources to essentially eradicate hookworm in the South. Likewise, religious groups have for centuries provided education in some of the poorest places in the world, providing an alternative to failing public schools.

Even the world's most problematic governments provide an opportunity for creative capitalists. Official government aid, or aid from the World Bank, must work through official channels. Even so, little of that aid reaches its intended recipients. Creative capitalists have the option of insisting, as Herbert Hoover did, that their aid will be administered free from the grabbing hand of the state.

Private groups with a public mission may also be one of the best ways to improve the quality of government. A large body of research has emerged to support the view that quality of government is itself a function of private social groups that prod for accountability, openness, and democracy. The freedom of Poland owes much to an internal private group (Solidarity) and an external philanthropic organization (the Catholic Church). And private philanthropists have often been effective counterweights against the excesses of local government within the U.S.

For creative capitalism to be most effective, it needs to recognize that profit-maximizing firms will not solve all of the world's problems on their own. But it is even more important to recognize the great failures of the public sector, especially in the developing world. The independence and resources of creative capitalists offer at least the possibility of redressing those failures.

BUT WAIT! CAN'T THE POOR DECIDE FOR THEMSELVES?

Gregory Clark

Bill Gates has two major points. His first is that the profit motive fails to provide goods, such as vaccines, that the poor of the third world need. His second point is that the solution to this problem is neither government action nor private philanthropy; the needs are too great. Instead, we need corporate action.

But despite Bill Gates's abundant good intentions, I have to dispute both propositions.

1. As Michael Kinsley points out, much of modern capitalism is characterized by firms with high fixed costs—for research and development, for production facilities—but low production costs. Think computer software, think computers, think drugs, think airplanes. This production structure, however, favors mostly third-world consumers.

True, they have little to spend. But such goods cost little to deliver to the third world once developed in high-income countries, because it costs little to produce more units. And the poor get served because the good old-fashioned profit motive says make a buck wherever you can.

It is only when the goods the third world desires differ from those of rich-country consumers that we have a problem. And although Bill Gates gives a rundown of such goods—antimalarial drugs are a prominent example—it is actually a short list. For a whole range of goods—clothing, cars, cell phones, electronics, computers, entertainment—the goods bought by the poorest overlap enough with those bought by the rich that there is little problem. They are indeed well served by selfish capitalism.

The cell phone is a great example. It is sweeping Africa, with affordable service on offer to people earning two dollars a day.

The call for corporate philanthropy toward the third world is thus redundant for many companies—companies like GM, Intel, Boeing, Monsanto, Wal-Mart, Universal Pictures, and Coca-Cola, to name a few. What would they develop that they do not already supply to the world's poor?

Where there is no such overlap between the consumption habits of the rich and poor worlds—as is the case with pharmaceuticals—the problem would be better handled by private philanthropy, where profits earned in any sector of the U.S. economy can be applied. Calling all U.S. companies to the third-world technological battlefront, no matter how ill equipped they are to contribute their expertise, just wastes resources.

2. A second problem with Gates's proposal is that it assumes that the poor of Africa do not know their own best interests. Instead, corporate America is thought to be a more discerning judge of those interests.

For example, the problem of orphan-drug development—

that is, developing drugs for diseases that afflict only a small number of people in the United States—arises because the poor do not have the income to make research and development sustainable. But if that is the case, why isn't the solution to have U.S. corporations give money directly to the poor? That way the poor can choose how they want to spend their charity: on vaccines or, if they prefer, on cell phones, on food, or even on beer.

Suppose it costs $100 million to develop a new vaccine for malaria, and suppose that a U.S. drug company, instead of developing the vaccine, gave $100 million directly to the African poor. If the poor viewed the vaccine as their top priority, then the $100 million transfer would raise vaccine demand enough to justify U.S. production. If, however, the African poor have other priorities, then they will spend the money on something other than the vaccine, and be better off for it.

My guess is that the third-world poor, if given their share of the money, would spend it on some more pressing priority than vaccination, like shelter or food. And in any case, Bill Gates's call for firms to do production directly without testing demand is a call to substitute the judgment of U.S. corporations for that of the third-world poor. That needs some more careful justification.

3. A third difficulty with Gates's proposal is that it works only in sectors where supernormal profits exist—sectors in which firms are worth much more than the replacement costs of their capital. (And such sectors will only accidentally correspond to sectors in which there is third-world need.) In competitive industries, like the modern airline industry, there are no surpluses available to direct toward the needs of the poor. Firms have to maximize profits just to stay in business. American Airlines can't help the poor of the third world stay alive when it is struggling to stay alive itself.

So reluctantly, I have to conclude that private philanthropy, not corporate activism, is a better way to help the world's poor.

LET OLD-FASHIONED CAPITALISM HELP THE POOR

William Easterly

Bill Gates's speech on creative capitalism was misguided in two important ways: It made a false accusation about traditional capitalism, and it made extravagant claims for corporate philanthropy.

The false accusation was that traditional capitalism fails to help the poor. It is certainly true that firms have much more incentive to meet the needs of rich people with money than to meet the needs of poor people without money. What Mr. Gates forgot was that as firms expand their production to meet more of rich people's needs, they hire more unskilled labor to do so—driving up the incomes of poor people. As firms invest in machines to increase production for the rich market, they drive up the productive power of workers, further increasing wages of poor people. And firms have an incentive to continually search for new technologies that make both machines and workers more productive, which once again—you guessed it—drives up the wages of the poor.

Think of the information revolution that makes today's factories more efficient—i.e., that makes both machines and workers more productive. Or, if you prefer historical examples, think of the assembly line, a new technology that simply rearranged machines and workers in a way that made them all more productive. Traditional capitalist forces like these explain why unskilled wages trend steadily upward and the poverty rate (measured at a fixed poverty line in real terms) has declined drastically in American history. Such forces also largely explain why the global poverty rate has fallen by half over the last three decades.

I am sympathetic to Gates's impatience that the fall in poverty is not fast enough and that global inequities are still too large. If I knew of a system that did better than traditional capitalism (I don't), I would be happy to join its advocacy campaign.

But Bill Gates's creative capitalism is not such a system. I am sympathetic to the case for corporate philanthropy, which I think Ed Glaeser articulates well. But Mr. Gates makes two implicit claims that don't withstand scrutiny. The first is that corporate philanthropy can exist on a large enough scale to make a dent in world poverty. Second is that corporate philanthropy is an effective and efficient vehicle for meeting the needs of poor people.

On the first claim: According to the Hudson Institute, American corporate philanthropy to the developing world was about $5.5 billion in 2006. U.S. GDP in 2006, on the other hand, was $13.4 trillion. Gates's concept of "recognition" as a reward may help increase that $5.5 billion, but current outcomes suggest that companies get enough recognition from relatively tiny amounts of corporate giving, compared to what they produce for markets. I don't see anything on the horizon that would drastically change that—not even an eloquent speech by Bill

Gates. Moral exhortation has a very limited effect on most people's behavior, much as we might wish it otherwise.

But even if the amount of corporate philanthropy were somehow drastically increased, would it be effective in meeting the needs of the poor? Philanthropy faces the same problem that has bedeviled foreign aid: Even if "recognition" does matter a little, you get the recognition for the gift itself, not for the gift's effect on the poor—which comes much later and is largely unseen by those who allocate "recognition."

You have to work very hard to figure out what the poor want and need, and you have to work very hard to meet those needs under local conditions. Corporate philanthropists would do well to draw on the entrepreneurial skills that made their corporations successful when they try to solve these difficult problems. Unfortunately, my experience so far with corporate social responsibility (CSR) departments is that they are too often filled with wooly-headed people hired especially for CSR— and not anyone with entrepreneurial experience from the corporation itself. This fits the theory that CSR departments have more incentive to do PR (that's all you need to get Mr. Gates's "recognition") than to achieve results for the poor.

Why does all of this matter? Political debate about which economic system to favor is still ongoing in much of the world—in countries both rich and poor. Mr. Gates's speech attacks the system that has historically done the most to alleviate poverty—traditional capitalism—in favor of an untried and implausible alternative, an illusory third way that mixes profits and altruism. The effect of such advocacy may be to increase job opportunities for aid bureaucrats—now they can work for CSR as well as for the World Bank!—but will decrease job opportunities for poor workers, as true capitalism retreats under political attack.

HOW CAPITALISM CAN REALLY GET CREATIVE

Steven Landsburg

Bill Gates has told us that: (1) capitalism is good and (2) a different kind of capitalism could be even better. I agree with both points, but I'd like to get clearer about the meanings of "different" and "better."

I take it that the goal is to eradicate poverty, as opposed to merely mitigating the worst depredations of poverty. To eradicate poverty, you must raise wages; to raise wages, you must make workers more productive. As Bill Easterly observed, productive workers need productive machinery, and that's where capitalism comes in. You can't end poverty without capitalism. (And indeed, prior to capitalism—more precisely, prior to the Industrial Revolution—the entire world was poor.)

Productive workers also need good health and good educations. These are areas where it might or might not be possible to do a lot of good outside the usual market mechanisms. These are empirical questions.

But the bottom line regarding poverty eradication is this: Capitalism is indispensable; health and education measures are a potential help. And if creative capitalism discourages the accumulation of capital—either directly, or, as Easterly points out, by dampening enthusiasm for traditional capitalism—then it's surely counterproductive.

If we're going to get creative, we should keep this pitfall in mind. Which leads me to this: Corporations do a lot of good things. They also do a lot of bad things, such as lobbying for trade restrictions or using the legal system to prevent other corporations from innovating. (Those trade restrictions in particular tend to disserve both the poorest people in the West and the poorest people in the world.) But if you encourage corporations to do more good (in the form of philanthropy and so on), then you detract from their primary mission. If you encourage corporations to do less bad, then you enhance their primary mission.

If Archer Daniels Midland wants to get creative, I'd like to see it abolish its lobbying arm and let the sugar quota expire. If the oil companies want to get creative, let them refuse on principle to accept subsidies for offshore oil drilling. Let the auto and steel industries announce that they will no longer lobby for tariffs or other forms of protection.

How do we effect these changes? I have no idea. I also have no idea how we could get any of these corporations to be more philanthropic. Either way, we need some creativity. But I'd like to see some of that creativity directed toward making markets work better, not circumventing them.

LET'S MOVE BEYOND
MILTON FRIEDMAN'S ICY PURITY

Ed Glaeser

Milton Friedman's "The Social Responsibility of Business" (the full text of which is reprinted on page 287 of the appendix) is a great essay, which reminds us that the anthropomorphic tendency to treat corporations as independent actors is an error. Corporations represent shareholders; their primary obligation is to enrich those shareholders. When corporate chieftains use their shareholders' money to support pet social causes, they are depriving those shareholders of the right to make their own charitable decisions—and they are taking credit with the largesse of their investors.

I believe strongly in the basic thrust of Friedman's argument. In many if not most cases, corporations should pay more attention to their shareholder responsibilities than to anything else. But the icy purity of Friedman's argument has always bothered me. Surely, we don't think that employees can really be autoprogrammed to serve only their investors' interests, do we? Humans like to think that we have some sort of higher purpose in our lives and in our work, even if it is just taking pride in building a well-crafted car or being a kind coworker. There is certainly honor in enriching one's backers, but I suspect that many would question whether this is really the best way to spend our short time on the planet.

The quest for meaning in life and work is, of course, something of a luxury good, which means that it has gotten more important over time as we have become richer. The only meaning that my grandfather saw or needed in his work was that it provided him with enough money to feed his family and send his children to college. Today, my students at Harvard generally expect a job that is both well paying and internally rewarding. Creative capitalism would help firms attract those students by making their work seem more socially worthwhile. Some corporate social responsibility is often in the shareholders' interests because it attracts a better group of workers, but too much honesty about that will just destroy the feeling of doing good.

Two years ago, Michael Keiser, one of the founders of Recycled Paper Greetings, spoke at a conference at the University of Chicago in honor of Friedman's great student Gary Becker. Recycled Paper Greetings was founded in 1971—during an era of booming social consciousness—and the founders hoped that the company's ecological ambitions would help attract consumers. As Keiser told it, consumers were pretty indifferent to the recycled nature of the paper cards, and the firm had to compete with Hallmark on price and quality. The environmentalist mission did more for them in attracting workers who valued being part of something with a higher purpose. Recycled Paper Greetings was able to attract and retain more dedicated employees by hewing to the firm's ecological mission.

Anyone who manages in a university or foundation or hospital knows that one of the comparative advantages of the nonprofit sector is that we believe we are doing good in the world. Cash can certainly motivate people, but so can other ideals. Just as armies moved from being purely mercenary affairs to being forces dedicated to honor and patriotism, I expect to see more and more companies embrace complex objectives that go beyond making money.

None of this negates Friedman's essential point that under current contract law, for-profit firms have a fiduciary duty to their shareholders that translates into an overwhelming legal and moral obligation. So if more corporations are going to be "creative," then we surely need to consider new contractual forms that reflect the fact that firms may want to do other things in addition to making money for their shareholders. For example, firms can certainly have two types of voting shares, one of which goes to investors and the other of which goes to workers. The legal obligation of the firm under this structure would be to return a decent profit to shareholders and to cater to their empowered workers' desire to do something good. This kind of dual responsibility is certainly messier than pure profit maximization, but if the legal form clearly empowered voters who didn't get dividends, then many of Friedman's objections would disappear. After all, the shareholders would know that they weren't getting aboard an enterprise with nothing but money on its mind.

Creative capitalism creates challenges for traditional governance structures, but those challenges are not insurmountable. They just require a bit of creativity.

WHY CREATIVE CAPITALISM
WOULD MAKE THINGS WORSE

Richard Posner

My reaction to "creative capitalism" as lauded by Bill Gates, Warren Buffett, Michael Kinsley, and (somewhat to my surprise) Professor Glaeser is sheer skepticism. The embrace of massive corporate charity, the criticism of capitalism by its greatest beneficiaries, the frequent resort by the advocates of "creative capitalism" to platitudes ("the world is getting better, but not fast enough and not for everyone"; "today's miracles of technology benefit only those who can afford them"; "economic demand is not the same as economic need"), and the vagueness of the term itself all leave me with an uncomfortable feeling.

Corporate managers have a fiduciary duty to maximize corporate profits. This duty does not exclude the possibility of corporate philanthropy, although the word "philanthropy" used in the context of profit maximization is misleading. Corporations have long made charitable donations, quite properly from a profit-maximizing standpoint, in order to curry favor with politicians and interest groups, advertise the corporation to potential consumers (as by underwriting cultural events), create diffuse goodwill, disguise greed, and ward off criticisms. Call this public relations (PR) charity. With the increase in economic inequality in the United States, and in particular the emergence of a tier of unbelievably wealthy businessmen, the pressure to take part in PR charity has increased. In addition, with increasing globalization, there is a growing incentive for another kind of profit-maximizing corporate charity—call it jump-start charity—in which charitable donations are directed to building future demand for the donor's product in poor countries.

This is particularly important with respect to products that involve network externalities—products like the telephone, where the value increases when more people use it—so that being first in a market may give one a head start that is difficult to overcome. The more people use Windows, the more valuable Windows is to other people. And once hooked on Windows, a person is likely to buy Microsoft's applications programs, such as Office. Because the marginal cost of an operating system is essentially zero, giving it away may be profit maximizing if it induces the purchase of applications programs that run on it and creates a network effect. But the giveaway can be advertised as philanthropic.

A corporation that makes charitable donations that are not profit maximizing is not only breaking faith with its shareholders (unless for some reason they unanimously support the diversion of corporate profits to the managers' preferred charities) but also weakening itself in competition with profit-maximizing firms. The "creative capitalism" movement equivocates on this point. Gates seems to argue that giving up profits is good business, primarily because it attracts idealistic young workers, presumably at a lower wage than what a pure profit maximizer would have to pay to overcome the idealism. (He also says that recognition for doing good "enhances a company's reputation and appeals to customers," but that is just PR charity and is consistent with unalloyed profit maximization.)

I doubt there are many such companies. But what may be true is that some of the charitable projects that Gates would like Microsoft and other big companies to pursue may be more interesting than some of the firms' pure business projects, and thus may provide nonpecuniary income to employees that would let the firm pay lower wages. There is an analogy here to pro bono work by law firms, which is attractive to young lawyers because it is more interesting than much of their ordinary work or at least provides welcome variety. Of course, if "creative capitalism" reduces labor costs by enough to offset the cost of a charitable undertaking, it is still consistent with strict profit maximization. But I am reluctant to attribute corporate philanthropy to altruism because altruism, outside the family, tends to be a very weak force compared to self-interest. Most people are largely indifferent to the suffering of people in remote countries unless that suffering is on TV.

Bill Gates and Warren Buffett believe that corporations are more efficient than foundations and government, and so if the charity function is turned over to the corporate sector it will be performed better. (Warren Buffett suggests semifacetiously that 3 percent of the revenue from the corporate income tax might be allocated to a fund "that would be administered by some representatives of corporate America to be used in intelligent ways for the long-term benefit of society.") But corporations are more efficient because they operate under the discipline of profit maximization, which will be dissipated if they direct significant resources to charitable projects. There is even a danger that altruistic corporations would exert pressure on the government to compel their nonaltruistic competitors to undertake charitable projects as well, in order to prevent those competitors from taking over the market.

And I am troubled by the emphasis that advocates of "creative capitalism" place on foreign charity centered on Africa. The problem of Africa is not a lack of money but political corruption and incompetence. We know this because China and India were able to lift themselves by their bootstraps once they got the rudiments of competent and market-friendly government in place, and because Africa's development slowed when the colonial governments were replaced by less efficient indigenous ones.

Foreign charity can actually worsen the quality of government in poor countries by reducing the pressure for reform. The creative capitalists seem oblivious to the problem. Their neglect seems related to a lack of interest in systematic data. At least in the literature of creative capitalism that I have read, I see no reference to evidence beyond the anecdotal that corporate philanthropy in Africa has produced net benefits for Africans. It is possible that efforts by businessmen of Bill Gates's caliber will succeed where governments and the World Bank have failed. But I would like to see some evidence—especially since the Gates Foundation and other private foundations compete with governments and the World Bank for staff, which may either weaken the charitable efforts of governments and foundations or make those efforts more expensive by increasing staffing costs, which amounts to the same thing.

I also wonder why rich Americans seem so eager to send their surplus money abroad. (Granted, the Gates Foundation also makes large domestic grants.) It is not as if the United States lacks appropriate objects of charity. Nor do I see any recognition of the downside of efforts to reduce poverty in Africa, a downside that extends well beyond strengthening the current rulers of African countries: increased demand for scarce commodities such as oil, increased carbon emissions, and overpopulation.

I am surprised to see Professor Glaeser saying that "while laissez-faire capitalism has worked many miracles, it has never been particularly well targeted towards righting social inequities. Private firms usually have better incentives to cater to the rich than to the poor." That is misleading. The incentive of private firms is to maximize profits, and they often do this by catering to the poor (not of course the absolutely indigent), who in the aggregate often have far more buying power than the rich. American industry has historically catered to middle- and lower-middle-class consumers, and the rich have bought imported luxuries. Henry Ford made the Model T, not the Rolls-Royce.

I also disagree with Glaeser that "the case for creative capitalism is based as much on the failures of government as on the failures of private business." The failures of government are the case against charity, because charity entrenches those failures by reducing pressure for reform. None of the examples that Glaeser gives of successful philanthropy—Hoover's American Relief Administration, Rockefeller's personal (not corporate) charities, Solidarity (not a philanthropic enterprise), or the Roman Catholic Church—illustrates corporate charity (or "creative capitalism"). Nor is it realistic to suppose that corporations will, as Glaeser hopes, be able to bypass corrupt governments. (Why would a corrupt government permit that?) I am also not persuaded by Glaeser's proposal for quasi–worker cooperatives in lieu of the conventional business corporation. Worker co-ops do not have a good record, and a hybrid version is unpromising.

CAN CORPORATIONS THAT DO GOOD REALLY COMPETE?

Gary Becker

My great teacher and close friend, the late Milton Friedman, took a well-known negative position on corporate responsibility. This is also the position taken by Richard Posner. But unlike Posner and Friedman, I do not see anything wrong with Gates, Buffett, and others encouraging corporations to be more concerned about goals other than profit. The real test is how viable such corporations will be in a market environment where the competition includes companies motivated only by profits.

In the past several decades, economists have analyzed the competition of companies motivated solely by the desire for profits against companies motivated in part by other considerations. These other considerations include altruism toward consumers, discrimination against minority employees, and a desire to help the environment. The main conclusion of this analysis is that companies that forgo some profits to pursue other goals have trouble competing against profit-maximizing firms. Take competition between firms that hire workers solely on the basis of their productivity and cost and companies that give up profits to avoid hiring African Americans or some other minority. Since firms interested only in profits will hire minority workers when that is profitable and prejudiced firms will not, the discriminating firms will operate under a competitive disadvantage.

Companies that combine the profit motive with environmental and other concerns can thrive in a competitive environment only if they are able to attract employees and customers who also value these other corporate goals. Then the added cost of pursuing nonprofit goals would be partially, if not entirely, offset by having customers who pay more for their products, such as fair-trade coffees. Or these companies may be able to attract high-level employees at a relatively low price because the employees are excited by the prospects of spending some of their working time helping others, perhaps by developing vaccines that can treat diseases common in poor countries. These appear to be the types of companies that Bill Gates wants at the forefront of his "creative capitalism."

How successful can this form of capitalism be? Gates quotes with approval the opening discussion in Adam Smith's outstanding 1759 book *The Theory of Moral Sentiments* on the importance of altruism in human motivation. But while this book does deal with motives like concern for others and the desire for recognition, Smith was skeptical not about the strength of altruism but about its scope or reach. At one point, Smith uses an example that is highly relevant to Gates's present quest: He asks "how a man of humanity in Europe" would respond to hearing "that the great empire of China . . . was suddenly swallowed up by an earthquake." Smith's answer was that if the man "was to lose his little finger tomorrow, he would not sleep tonight; but, provided he never saw [the people of China] he would snore with the most profound security over the ruin of a hundred million of his brethren, and the destruction of that immense multitude seems plainly an object less interesting to him than this paltry misfortune of his own."

Globalization has brought the situations in China, India, Africa, and other poor parts of the world much closer to the concerns of men and women in rich countries than they could ever have been in Smith's time. Still, essentially for the reasons Smith gives, it would be quite difficult to get many companies in richer countries to be highly motivated by a desire to cure third-world diseases. It would not be any easier to get companies to spend significant resources to lower carbon emissions, unless these expenditures were forced by governments or compensated by public or private sources.

But while it is very difficult for companies to pursue such goals when they face competitors driven solely by profits, a monopolist can pursue other goals and forfeit profits, even when stockholders object (although private equity companies or corporate raiders may try to replace the management team with one motivated solely by profit considerations). And it is not clear that the economy is worse off when management of a monopoly uses some of its extra profits to pursue environmental and other nonprofit goals. In the short run, its stockholders would suffer from not getting full monopoly returns, but others might benefit from such behavior. In the long run, the stockholders of monopoly companies would receive the risk-adjusted competitive rate of return on their capital, regardless of what management does.

Even so, there are far more effective ways than corporate philanthropy to help poor nations speed up their economic development and reduce the impact of malaria, AIDS, and other devastating diseases. Probably the single most important step is to encourage more competition and market-friendly policies. As Richard Posner points out, corporate philanthropy and especially government aid has probably slowed the introduction of such reforms. And it would help to reduce—or, better still, eliminate—the tariffs that rich countries impose on agricultural and other imports from developing countries.

A Reply to Richard Posner:
REFORM COMES FROM THE BOTTOM UP
Ed Glaeser

Posner writes that he is "not persuaded by Glaeser's proposal for quasi–worker cooperatives in lieu of the conventional business corporation." But I never suggested, or thought, that there would be widespread replacement of conventional firms with "quasi–worker cooperatives." My point was that there are a lot of workers, and entrepreneurs, with all sorts of goals that aren't exactly conventional profit maximization. Trying to insert those goals into a conventional corporation seems like a mistake, for all the reasons that Friedman eloquently details. It is far better for firms to keep to their fiduciary duty of enriching their stockholders.

Today, if entrepreneurs and workers want some alternative type of firm, there is only one primary contractual form to accommodate them: not-for-profit organizations. These organizations can, of course, borrow and solicit donations, but they can't issue equity.

It seems reasonable to enrich the contract space so that there are hybrid firms that combine their financial obligations to investors with other social objectives. I suspect that such hybrid firms will always be a small part of the economy and that many will fail, but I don't see a downside to allowing experimentation in this area.

Furthermore, I disagree with the view that the track record of such hybrid firms is so dismal. Much of the nonprofit world looks like such a hybrid—a workers' cooperative. Not-for-profit hospitals, famously called "physicians' cooperatives," are one example. There are also for-profit firms, like the Ford Motor Company, where the shareholders bought in knowing full well that controlling rights would be lodged in the hands of the company's founding family and that this family might not always maximize profits.

The larger point of disagreement between Judge Posner and myself concerns the role that independent actors can play in the process of political reform in the developing world. I agree with him that the problems of sub-Saharan Africa are fundamentally political and that political change is the most important development need. My view, with which he may not agree, is that this political change must consist of governments that: (1) protect property rights and (2) invest in human capital (both education and health). The big question is: How does such political change come about?

Judge Posner seems to have a model in mind where sufficient deprivation creates pressure for reform and then good things happen. I don't think that this is what the history of reform looks like. The correlation between democracy and income is, after all, strongly positive, and Robert Barro and others have suggested that higher incomes produce a higher chance of sustaining democracy, rather than the other way around. I know of no evidence to suggest that keeping people poor makes reform more likely.

My own view is that reform comes from the bottom up—from people and organizations that have the resources to create change. Education makes political activists more effective, and I think this is one reason why education seems to be a necessary ingredient in sustainable democracies. Independent organizations also seem to play a role in creating a functioning democracy, at least if we accept political scientist Robert Putnam's evidence.

Many of the world's poorest nations are notably short on both strong private organizations and education. The intervention of independent organizations with a relatively benign agenda could make up for the weaknesses of homegrown organizations. Any outside "charity" that helps build human capital will, I think, make reform more likely. Corrupt governments won't naturally want to cooperate with these groups, but at the right price, they will.

A final issue is the comparability between "creative capitalism" and the social organizations like the Catholic Church, which I mentioned in my original post. At this point, I really have no idea what these "creative capitalist" organizations will look like. Moreover, I don't know what types of organizations will be effective in the future. In more hopeful moments, I can imagine that these organizations might end up being quite helpful, and I would guess that they will evolve until they become more effective. Given the depths of poverty in sub-Saharan Africa, I have trouble imagining that they could make things worse.

A Reply to Ed Glaeser:

WHAT KIND OF FIRM ARE WE TALKING ABOUT?

Richard Posner

I can't picture the kind of firm that Professor Glaeser has in mind. That may just be a lack of imagination on my part. It seems he envisions a charity that issues equity but with no voting rights. Presumably, the equity investors would themselves be altruistically motivated, since they would get a below-market return. Wouldn't they prefer to make an outright donation and invest their money elsewhere? What do they gain by bundling charity and income? Wouldn't they lose their tax deduction? Is *The New York Times* the kind of hybrid he is recommending? It is surely a mess.

I agree that average incomes and political stability are positively correlated (and have argued as much elsewhere), but I do not agree that charity promotes democracy. A dictatorship will accept foreign aid, public or private, only in forms that do not threaten its control; we're seeing this in Zimbabwe. Education can be a mode of indoctrination. Nazi Germany, Soviet Russia, and Castro's Cuba all made education a national priority.

And I do not understand the basis of Glaeser's optimism about "creative capitalism" when he says that he has "no idea what these 'creative capitalist' organizations will look like."

IS CREATIVE CAPITALISM ILLEGAL?

John Quiggin

I have a couple of problems with Richard Posner's notion of fiduciary obligation—the idea that firms are obligated to act in the interest of stockholders or, more specifically in Posner's formulation, to maximize corporate profits.

First, what is meant by "obligation"? The obvious interpretation is that fiduciary obligation exists under statutory or judge-made corporate law. But if this were the main reason for arguing that firms should maximize profits, the solution would be simple: change the law so that companies are free to take a broader range of goals into account. Such a change would be less than earth shattering: in many countries, such as Germany, companies are obliged to take worker interests into account, and capitalism does not appear to have collapsed as a result. But I somehow doubt that, if U.S. law were changed to remove any obligation to maximize profits (to create an obligation to pursue broader social goals), Posner's objections to creative capitalism would be dissolved.

That's because there is a second definition of "obligation": Posner argues that managers have an obligation to "keep faith" with shareholders. His argument is that if a company issues equity under the implied assumption that its managers will maximize profits, and then decides today to pursue other goals, shareholders can reasonably argue that an implicit contract has been broken. On the other hand, much of the corporate history of the U.S. since the 1970s has consisted of the repudiation of implicit contracts with workers, and they have found little redress. And in any case, such problems don't arise for new companies, who state their policies at the outset.

So, presumably, the broadest argument in favor of profit maximization must rely on enlightened self-interest: Posner and others argue, plausibly enough, that a company that doesn't maximize profits is weakening itself in competition with other firms. To be more precise, the probability of bankruptcy or hostile takeover presumably is increased by deviations from profit maximization. But this doesn't mean that the probability of a firm's survival is maximized by maximizing profits. Socially concerned executives and managers might well decide that a company strategy of incorporating broad social goals is the best way to maximize their own payoff—including the risk of driving the company out of business.

If an argument is to be made against creative capitalism, fiduciary obligation seems like a very weak reed. A better way of approaching the question would be to ask whether the goals of all concerned might better be met if managers ran companies to maximize profits and then used their own wealth to pursue social goals. This is, broadly speaking, what Gates has done. It's the Bill & Melinda Gates Foundation, not the Microsoft Corporation, that is fighting malaria.

But it's far from clear that this neat separation will always apply. Pharmaceutical corporations, for example, face large fixed costs in developing medicines and low marginal costs in producing them. This situation creates a great deal of scope for different pricing regimes: as others have argued, it's easy to describe cases where the socially optimal price is going to be very different from that which maximizes profits.

And it may well be that behaving as a good corporate citizen is conducive to long-term survival. This isn't just a matter of buying PR with customers, as Posner suggests. If political actors generally regard the activities of a firm as socially desirable, they will presumably be less likely to take action that might damage it. And while political perceptions do not always coincide with social reality, it's hard to believe, in global terms, that the strategies adopted by major pharmaceutical companies in recent decades have been either socially optimal or tailored to maximize the probability that the industry will survive in the long term in anything like its current form.

CAN A CORPORATION DO GOOD WITHOUT FEAR OF CARL ICAHN?

Ronald J. Gilson

(An email exchange with Michael Kinsley)

FROM MIKE TO RON:

Let me rephrase the question that has come up, to which we need an answer. (No doubt I learned the answer in law school, but thirty years later I haven't a clue.) Is the corporation's fiduciary duty to maximize profits for shareholders hardwired into corporate law, or is it something a corporation could opt out of in its bylaws or wherever? I.e., could a corporation put the world, including all potential stockholders, on notice: We do not maximize profits. We aim for X percent and then give the rest to charity. Or we don't lay off employees even in bad times, or we let our scientists spend 20 percent of their time curing malaria. Or whatever. And could it do this without fear of Carl Icahn?

FROM RON TO MIKE:

The answer to your question turns out to be a little complicated, mostly because the question has to be a lot more precise.

To give you an example, as a practical matter corporate managers are almost entirely free from the risk of legal sanctions that would follow from being more sympathetic to workers, or to the community, or to the environment, than hypothetical shareholder maximization would dictate, as long as the managers are willing to be a little duplicitous. Almost anything can be justified as in the corporation's long-run best interests, and courts, under the guise of the business judgment rule, will not second-guess the managers' rationalization.

Given that wide range of operating discretion, is there any check on management's ability to disregard shareholder value? The answer is the capital market—if managers diverge so far from shareholder profit maximization that a hostile tender offer or a proxy fight is a sound investment, then here comes Icahn. (I was part of Icahn's dissident slate the first time he tried the proxy fight route, years ago, trying to make U.S. Steel spin off Marathon Oil; he was right but gave up.) At that point, the legal issue turns to defensive tactics. Most of the fights over the years have been over what managers could do to defend their discretion without shareholder approval. (If shareholders would approve defensive measures, then they also wouldn't tender, so there really was no issue.) The poison pill—a purposely intolerable provision triggered by a takeover offer—was the best example of this behavior: the key to Marty Lipton's diabolical machine is that shareholders do not have to approve the adoption of a pill and maybe—the issue is still open—cannot cause it to be redeemed except by removing a majority of the board.

That's where things stand without special charter provisions. The next step is Google (or *The New York Times*, or *The Washington Post*, or, outside the U.S., Investor AG in Sweden) where founders retain voting control through two classes of common stock, the one with controlling voting rights being kept by the founders, even if they no longer have a majority of the economic interest. This does not change the basic rule that managers have to talk as if they are maximizing long-term shareholder value, but it does foreclose the operation of capital market discipline when they go too far.

That gets us, finally, to your question: Can altruistic founders be honest by including in the corporate charter a provision that allows them to maximize something other than shareholder values? (It is a different but not interesting question from your perspective whether the provision has to be in the charter or can be in the bylaws, since you are assuming founders will put it in the right document when they form the venture. In some states—Indiana and Pennsylvania, for example—the corporate law is explicit that managers do not have to maximize shareholder value. These provisions were adopted to provide antitakeover protection and no one really knows what they mean, because it remains easier to rationalize what you are doing than openly defend it.) The short answer, I think, is that you can certainly include such a provision in the charter with specialized Delaware entities, like LLCs [limited liability companies] and limited partnerships, and likely can do it with a normal corporation, subject to background rules against self-dealing.

But that formulation seems to me to suggest that you are asking the wrong question. Who would buy something if they did not know how much of the income was going to be diverted from the shareholder value to, say, the stakeholder value? If one knows the limits, then it is easy: The price will be discounted until the returns are equivalent between stakeholder- and shareholder-maximizing companies. If one does not know the limits, then why would anyone—whether greedy or altruistic—invest? Profit seekers would prefer a shareholder-maximizing entity. Altruistic investors would be better off contributing to charities.

In the end, I am not convinced that "creative capitalism" has a great deal more content than "compassionate conservatism." As a thought problem, would you rather have a stakeholder-oriented company or the same funds directed to what people like Paul Brest, president of the Hewlett Foundation and former dean of Stanford Law School, are calling venture philanthropy?

This is an interesting set of issues, but in my experience, the debate is fuzzy because the question is never precisely framed. If you could frame the issues clearly enough that people actually had to address each other, it would be a great project. The danger is that when the issue is left fuzzy, everyone is free to avoid the difficult parts of their positions.

TEN POINTS ABOUT PROFIT

Martin Wolf

What is the goal of the limited liability, joint-stock company, the core institution of the contemporary capitalist economy? What implications does the answer have for such a company's freedom to be "creative" in the way Bill Gates uses the term? The classic answer to the first of these questions, repeated often in these discussions, is that its aim is to maximize profits. This statement is not false. But it is vastly too limited. Here are ten points relevant to this theme.

First, one has to distinguish the goal of the firm from its role. The role of companies is to provide valuable goods and services—that is to say, outputs worth more than their inputs. The great insight of market economics is that they will do this job best if they are subject to competition. Profit maximization (or shareholder value maximization, its more sophisticated modern equivalent) is *not* the role of the firm. It is its goal. The goal of profit maximization drives the firm to fulfill its role.

Second, by creating a competitive market for corporate control, we more or less force companies to maximize shareholder value or at least behave in ways that the market believes will lead them to do so. If companies fail to oblige, the company will be put "into play." Thus, in Anglo-American shareholder-driven capitalism, maximization of shareholder value (as perceived by the market) must perforce be the goal of the company. This is not the case in countries where a market in corporate control does not exist. In such countries, companies must earn a high enough return on capital to survive. But this need not be a shareholder value maximizing return.

Third, a company is viewed in the Anglo-American world as a bundle of contracts. But companies are also social organisms created by a highly gregarious mammalian species with a unique capacity for large-scale cooperation over time and space. Companies have cultures and histories. For many of those most closely associated with them, they also have (and offer) a certain meaning. Committed workers in successful companies do not work in order to maximize shareholder value or even to earn the largest possible living. Indeed, it is impossible to direct most companies solely by the goal of profit maximization. (Goldman Sachs may be an exception.) They have to be aimed at the intermediate goal of producing and developing goods and services that people want to buy and are worth more in the market than they cost to produce.

Fourth, the idea that a company is an entity that can be freely bought and sold is culturally specific. It is the view, above all, of Anglo-Americans. It is not shared in most of the rest of the world. The reason for this divergence is that, for many cultures, a company is viewed as being an enduring social entity. I once read that, for many Japanese, one can no more sell a company over the heads of its workers than one can sell one's grandmother. In this view, goods and services can be bought and sold. Companies, like countries (or, as we all now agree, people), must not be.

In this perspective, shareholders are not genuine owners. They contribute nothing of value to the competitive strengths of the firm, enjoy the benefits of limited liability, and are well able to diversify the risks they run. They are merely an (ever-shifting) group of people with a claim to the residual income. Those with the biggest (undiversifiable) investment in the firm—and thus the greatest exposure to firm-specific risks—are not shareholders but core workers. The interests of the latter are, therefore, paramount.

Fifth, the salient characteristic of the contracts inside the firm (that is, between the company, its employees, and, quite often, its suppliers and even distributors) is that they are relational. That is to say, they cannot be written down in any precise form. Companies are hierarchies in which people engage voluntarily. They necessarily work on the basis of trust in what is often a very long-term relationship: I work extra hard to meet a deadline now, in return for consideration when I need to look after my elderly mother later on. For many companies, trustworthiness is an essential ingredient in their long-term success.

Sixth, if companies can be freely bought and sold, relational contracts, which depend on continuing interaction among specific people inside the business, are hardly worth the paper they are (not) written on. Rational employees will act opportunistically, because they will always expect their company to do the same. The longer and more reliable relationships are expected to be, the less likely such opportunistic behavior is to emerge.

Seventh, accordingly, capital-market arrangements that enforce shareholder value maximization may (I stress "may") make companies work less efficiently than otherwise, by precluding long-term relationships between the firm and valuable employees.

Eighth, it is not necessarily even the case that companies that operate under the assumption that they can be bought and sold (like GM) will operate more successfully in terms of maximizing shareholder value than those that do not (such as Toyota). Toyota is a better car company than GM in almost all dimensions. Whatever the failures of Japanese capitalism, they cannot be blamed on the absence of an active market in corporate control.

Ninth, consequently, the room for enduring divergence in the forms of capitalism is bigger than those working in the Anglo-American intellectual tradition appreciate. In particular, without an active market for corporate control, management rules companies and acts as a trustee for a range of stakeholders, of whom core workers are the most important. Because these companies cannot be forced to maximize shareholder value, they can indeed undertake a range of costly "charitable" activities, provided they do not threaten the company's ability to survive.

Tenth, one of the most interesting questions over the next generation is whether the Anglo-American form of capitalism, which gives primary direction of companies to capital markets, will flourish and expand or not. Some of the evidence on the ineffectiveness of takeovers and the recent sad experiences in financial markets rather suggests not.

CAN YOU BE CREATIVE AND STILL BE CAPITALIST?

Matthew Bishop

A common theme in these critiques of creative capitalism is that, while "traditional" capitalism is the best bet for helping the poor, it is tragically impeded by the failure of government—the failure to provide rule of law, property rights, and protection against corruption. There is something to this argument. But is it really incompatible with creative capitalism?

The problem with simply blaming the governments in developing countries is that it is no help to the people living under those governments. Should selfish capitalists just sit back and wait until the politics of Africa change before they start raking in profits off the "next billion" or even the "bottom billion" customers?

That would be the wrong response from profit-maximizing companies because it would amount to a huge amount of lost profit in every year that those billions stay poor—not to mention other direct costs if the poverty creates revolution or conflict that spills over into other countries or the global economy.

Corporations and capitalism do not exist in a vacuum; they

thrive where the right rules of the game are in place. Corporations are "embedded" within societies. To improve their long-term profitability, embedded companies need to acknowledge and interact with the environment in which they operate and work to make that environment more hospitable. Poverty and deprivation each present both a lost opportunity and a threat to the social stability of capitalism. It might, therefore, be a rational long-term profit maximization strategy for companies to sacrifice some short-term profit to invest in "creative" or "socially responsible" or "philanthropic" activities that can make a country a more fruitful place for capitalism.

This begs a question: Can corporations be effective change agents in poorly governed countries, or can better governance be delivered only by the governments of rich countries, multilateral organizations, or nonprofits? Intuitively, there seems to be no reason why governments and nonprofits should have a monopoly on social innovation, especially as many wealthy governments now struggle to meet their existing social obligations. Nonprofits, too, are often focused on short-term fundraising to such an extent that they struggle to make long-term commitments to solving deep social problems.

In *Philanthrocapitalism,* Michael Green and I argue that big private philanthropies (such as the Bill & Melinda Gates Foundation) and big business have crucial, though subtly different, roles to play in addressing today's big social challenges. Both big business and big philanthropy are able to drive social change on a scale that smaller organizations and individuals cannot. Philanthropists are freer in how they use this agency, because unlike business they are not constrained by the need for long-run profitability. But business has capabilities—including global supply chains, distribution networks, and an abundance of high-quality human capital—that philanthropists often do not. Both can shape a society in ways that increase the ability of capitalism to lift the world's poor out of poverty.

Adam Smith's comment about our daily bread resulting not from the baker's benevolence but from his self-interest needs to be amended for the modern era, an era in which village bakeries have been replaced by multinational food giants with the ability to shape the societies in which they are embedded, for better or worse. Certainly, self-interest is the best way to put bread on poor people's tables, but enlightened self-interest by creative capitalists can potentially put better bread on more tables faster. The debate about "creative capitalism" should focus on the details of what can or should be done, not on whether it makes sense in principle.

WHY CREATIVE CAPITALISM GETS IN THE WAY OF DEMOCRACY

Robert Reich

I admire Bill Gates's attempt to put a human face on capitalism and make it work for the social good. But to the extent the project requires that capitalists sacrifice profits, it's doomed—as it should be in a democratic society.

The upsurge of interest in "corporate social responsibility" is related to a decreasing confidence in our democracy's responsiveness to the common good. Yet there is little reason to believe that corporations will be more responsive. After all, a major reason for democracy's failure is the overwhelming dominance of business lobbyists in the legislative process. Why would the same corporations that block legislative action on, say, the environment, voluntarily embark upon their own efforts to improve the environment?

Cynicism about democracy can also become a self-fulfilling prophecy, diverting attention from reforming it and deluding the public into believing that our common challenges are being adequately addressed by the private sector and therefore do not require public action. The soothing promise of corporate social responsibility can deflect public attention from the need for stricter laws and regulations or convince the public that there's no real problem to begin with. Politicians are simultaneously let off the hook. They can applaud some seeming act of corporate virtue—they may even take credit for pushing corporations to sign pledges or promise change—while not having to take any action that might cause negative reaction in boardrooms or among corporate fund-raisers. They don't have to take sides, or take a stand, while appearing to be in favor of virtuous corporate behavior.

Commitments to corporate social responsibility are also conveniently reassuring to talented or privileged young people who want both the sky-high financial rewards of fast-track executive careers and the psychological rewards of doing some good in the world. Rather than labor in the impecunious vineyards of social work or teaching school in a poor community, or public service in general, they can get their MBA and thereafter attach themselves to a big corporation that issues an annual report on all the good things it does for society. They can thereby do well and do good at the same time, or so they tell themselves.

But viewed this way, the term "corporate social responsibility" is as meaningful as cotton candy. The more you try to bite into it, the faster it dissolves. Absent a democratic process for articulating and enforcing public values, "social responsibility" has no inherent definition. Is nuclear energy socially responsible? Some environmentalists think nuclear energy is the best practical alternative to fossil-based fuels; others vehemently oppose it. Is it socially responsible to produce eggs from free-range hens, as some animal-rights advocates urge? Many food-safety advocates prefer that hens be caged in order to avoid contact with migratory birds that may carry avian flu. Should socially responsible investors and consumers eschew companies that produce any alcohol product, including beer or wine, or just hard liquor? Should they avoid media companies that produce any sexual or violent content, or just those that cross some threshold of indecency? Are companies that support gay rights and gun ownership being socially responsible or socially irresponsible?

Electoral democracy is messy and difficult, to be sure. Yet there is no means of determining the social obligations of the private sector other than through it. The goal of making companies more "socially responsible" would be better served by making democracy work better. Even if no consensus is possible, the democratic process and courts at least provide means of weighing and balancing claims. Not so in the private sector.

One popular argument is that "socially responsible" companies do better by their consumers and investors. Dow Chemical reduces its carbon emissions so it can lower its energy costs. McDonald's employs more humane slaughtering techniques, which prevent costly worker injuries and yield more meat. Wal-Mart has adopted "green" packaging for its fresh produce—transparent plastics made from corn sugars—because it's cheaper than petroleum-based packaging. Starbucks gives its part-time employees health insurance because that reduces employee turnover and helps its bottom line. Alcoa estimates annual savings of about $100 million from reduced energy use and related environmental improvements.

All these steps may be worthwhile, but they are not undertaken because they are socially responsible. They're done to reduce costs. To credit these corporations with being "socially responsible" is to stretch the term to mean anything a company might do to increase profits if, in doing so, it also happens to have some beneficent impact on the rest of society.

For many years, I have preached that social responsibility and profitability converge over the long term. That's because a firm that respects and values employees, the community, and the environment eventually earns the respect and gratitude of employees, the community, and the larger society—which eventually helps the bottom line. But I've never been able to prove this proposition nor find a study that confirms it. More important, from the standpoint of the modern firm, the long term may be irrelevant. Under supercompetitive capitalism— where entry barriers are rapidly dropping and every firm is under more competitive pressure than ever—the "long term" is the present value of future earnings. There is no better measure of this than share price.

Similarly, when the extra benefits of some product accrue to consumers individually, they may be willing to pay more for it. But this doesn't make the product "socially responsible," either. Energy-efficient appliances that save consumers money, organic foods that make them feel healthier, gourmet ice cream that's tastier because it's made with cream from cows with access to lots of pasture, salmon that's more delectable because it was caught in the wild rather than brought up in pens, and free-range eggs that make consumers feel more secure against salmonella may all be worth the higher price consumers pay for them. But consumers don't pay extra because of any presumed social good; they pay because it's worth it to them personally.

By the same token, companies that pay good wages and offer good benefits in order to attract and retain high-caliber employees are not being "socially responsible"; they are merely practicing good management. In general, corporate initiatives that improve the quality of products without increasing their price, or increase efficiency and productivity so that prices can be lowered, or otherwise generate higher profits and higher returns for investors, are not socially virtuous. They're just good management practices that should—and, given the intensifying competitive pressures they're under—will be undertaken regardless of how much or how little they benefit society.

To be sure, some consumers who are concerned about the social practices of the firms may skew their purchases toward those they deem socially responsible, and some investors equally concerned about corporate morality may park their savings in what are called "socially responsible investment" funds, which screen out certain offensive industries. But evidence shows that a very small number of consumers or investors actually do so. After an exhaustive review of the data, my colleague Professor David Vogel, of the Haas Business School at the University of California at Berkeley, concluded that "the social and environmental practices of the vast majority of companies have not had any demonstrated effects on their sales." For example, according to one wide-ranging study, consumers buy environmentally friendly products only when they cost no more than regular products, have at least the same level of quality and performance, come from a brand they know and trust, can be purchased at stores where they already shop, and don't require a significant change in habits to use.

It is much the same with investors. In 2004, total shares under the management of such funds made up less than 2 percent of mutual fund shares outstanding in the U.S. stock market. In Europe, socially responsible mutual funds account for an even lower portion—about a third of 1 percent. If such funds outperformed regular mutual funds, more investors would be drawn to them, but their record is decidedly mixed. Besides, most "socially responsible" fund portfolios include just about every large company featured in a typical mutual fund portfolio.

Many investors are interested in better corporate governance. But, ironically, better governance makes a firm more responsive to its investors—not to its employees, communities, or society as a whole. The more beholden CEOs and other top executives are to investors, the more likely they are to slash payrolls in pursuit of higher profits, uproot themselves from their traditional communities and rely on global supply chains instead, subject workers in developing nations to unsafe or unhealthy conditions, and pillage the environment—if these and other such antisocial techniques increase profits and share prices.

Hence, if we believe that the private sector should act on social values, we need strong democracies to articulate those values and reflect them in laws and rules. Yet vivid pronouncements and displays of corporate social responsibility can lull the public into believing those values are being addressed without government action, thereby masking the very problems democracy should grapple with—would grapple with—if the public understood their true dimensions.

In light of rumblings from the Federal Communications Commission and from conservative legislators concerned about sex and violence on the screen, cable operators in early 2006 announced plans to offer packages of family-friendly channels so parents could shield their children. This was sufficient to preempt legislative action. But the companies had made similar promises before that had never been fulfilled.

Presumably, cable companies will continue to pump out sex and violence until Congress or the FCC stops them, because sex and violence make money.

To take another example, several large food companies recently announced they would stop advertising certain products to children under the age of twelve. The news was hailed as a glowing example of corporate social responsibility. It was no such thing. A government study released before they made their move concluded that advertising directed toward children contributes to child obesity; two bills in Congress proposed that such advertising be regulated. The companies' initiative provided sufficient reassurance to the public that the bills never made it through Congress. But the firms remained conspicuously vague about how they defined healthy lifestyles or how such ads might compare to the presumably unhealthy lifestyles they would promote with the other half of their advertising budgets.

In recent years, politicians have got into something of a habit of publicly shaming companies that have acted badly in some way. Offending executives are typically hauled before congressional committees, where members of Congress berate them. But little legislation emerges to force the companies to behave any differently in the future. The public scoldings allow politicians to maintain good relations with the same companies and industries—collecting campaign donations, enjoying rounds of golf with their executives, tapping their corporate lobbyists for miscellaneous favors—while showing the public they're being "tough" on the wrongdoers. The public is led to believe that democracy is working when all that's really working is public relations.

Consider the public firestorm that ensued after Yahoo! decided in 2005 to surrender to Chinese authorities the names of Chinese dissidents who had used Yahoo! email. Google created for the Chinese authorities a censored version of its search engine, removing such incendiary words as "human rights" and "democracy." Microsoft removed blogs the Chinese government didn't like, and Cisco peddled its equipment to the Chinese police. Given that China is on the verge of becoming the world's largest internet market and that the Chinese government determines access to this market, the moves by these companies were understandable in competitive terms. None of these companies broke American law at the time. And apart from their duty to obey the law, corporate executives are not authorized by anyone—least of all by their consumers or investors—to balance profits against the public good. Nor do they have any expertise in making such moral calculations. That's why we live in a democracy, which is supposed to represent the public in drawing such lines. So the question Congress needed to address was whether American high-tech companies should be barred from cooperating with dictatorial governments to abridge human rights, even if this means losing business.

The House Subcommittee on Human Rights held hearings in February 2006, to which executives of these companies were summoned. The members berated them for what their companies had done, and the scoldings became headlines the next day. But Congress enacted no legislation.

Politics is also subverted when politicians ask corporations to take some action voluntarily in the public interest. The public is led to believe that a major problem—the need for millions of dollars in relief for the victims of a hurricane or tsunami, for example—is being addressed. Yet corporations can at most provide a relatively small portion of what's needed.

Corporations are not set up to be public charities. Shareholders do not entrust their money to corporate executives for them to give it away. The world's biggest philanthropists, Bill and Melinda Gates, do not draw on Microsoft's profits; they draw on their own wealth. The only legitimate reason for a corporation to be generous with its shareholders' money is to burnish its brand image, and such a rationale will go only so far. In the aftermath of Hurricane Katrina, Wal-Mart's CEO was candid about the limits of his firm's generosity. "We can't send three trailer loads of merchandise to every group that asks for it," he said, turning down a request for two thousand blankets. "We have to, at the end of this, have a viable business." Charitable giving by corporations is infinitely small compared to what the public sector dispenses.

The message that companies are moral beings with social responsibilities diverts public attention from the task of establishing laws and rules in the first place. The praise or blame for a company's behavior is soon forgotten and barely affects the behavior of consumers or investors.

Meanwhile, increasingly, the real democratic process is being left to companies and their lobbyists. If "corporate social responsibility"—or even "creative capitalism"—is to have any real meaning in the future, it is for companies to refrain from flooding Washington and any other seat of government with so many lobbyists and campaign contributions as to stymie democracy.

NO, CREATIVE CAPITALISM WILL ONLY MAKE DEMOCRACY STRONGER

Paul Ormerod

Academics should be feeling pretty pleased with this debate, regardless of the position they take. Men who have made stupendous amounts of money seem to really, really want to be remembered for the profundity of their thoughts rather than their mere financial success. Mr. Gates, with his concept of creative capitalism, joins Mr. Soros, with his invention of "reflexivity."

Both appear to subscribe to Keynes's famous aphorism that "The ideas of economists and political philosophers, both when they are right and when they are wrong, are more powerful than is commonly understood. Indeed the world is ruled by little else. Practical men, who believe themselves to be quite exempt from any intellectual influence, are usually the slaves of some defunct economist." So the way to be remembered is to have a Great Idea.

Mr. Gates's idea stands up rather better than that of Mr. Soros. Indeed, in it we can see reflections of it in Keynes's 1933 remark that "The decadent international but individualistic capitalism in the hands of which we found ourselves after the war is not a success. It is not intelligent. It is not beautiful. It is not just. It is not virtuous."

Capitalism faces a similar problem of legitimacy now, and it is this problem that I believe Mr. Gates is attempting to address. When Keynes wrote, output in America had just fallen by 30 percent. There were millions of unemployed living at near-starvation levels in the richest country in the world.

Yes, we have moved on enormously since then. The cornucopia which capitalism was to unleash in the second half of the twentieth century seemed barely conceivable in the immediate aftermath of the war. But there are profound—and perfectly reasonable—misgivings about the reward structure of contemporary capitalism. Financial capital has created a crisis, and no one, least of all the bankers themselves, knows how deep this crisis will be.

Yet the risk/reward structure in the industry has been wholly asymmetrical. The expensive Mayfair and Central Park apartments, the country seats in the Cotswolds, the mansions in the Hamptons—these will still belong to the bankers, even if they are made unemployed. The problem is that millions of others might be as well. In any event, the rebuilding of banks' balance sheets can take place only at the expense of the public sector. Everyone else pays for the bankers' mistakes.

This would not really matter if there were not, exactly as in the 1930s, a much more sinister rival political and economic system on offer to the developing nations of the world. As we know, markets and democracy are much better at delivering prosperity—in its widest sense—than central planning and authoritarianism. Yet it did not seem like that in the 1930s, when the supposed success of the Soviet Union contrasted with the apparent decadence of capitalism. Now we have, as America's main rival, China, controlled by a regime that has slaughtered, by various means, the best part of 100 million of its own citizens.

Mr. Gates is really calling for a general reevaluation of business ethics. It is not true to say that, if such a reevaluation were to happen, capitalism and the workings of markets would automatically be compromised and impeded. Scarcely a market in the history of the world has operated under the blessing of unconstrained profit maximization.

I think it is quite unfair for William Easterly to dismiss Gates's plea by writing that "Moral exhortation has a very limited effect on most people's behavior." The moral code of capitalism's elite is not built on any set of simple incentives.

Our knowledge of how behavior and attitudes either spread or are contained across networks has increased enormously in the past decade. In markets where social interaction is important, where tastes and preferences can be altered directly by the behavior of others, moral exhortation can swamp the immediate impact of monetary incentives. So, for example, the more CEOs who reject huge contractual bonuses when their company underperforms—as Willie Walsh at British Airways has recently done—the more likely it becomes that others will follow suit. It is not guaranteed, but it becomes more likely.

Of course, we know that these types of networks tend to be robust but fragile. "Robust" in the sense that the prevailing attitudes and behaviors are fairly sturdy in the face of small disturbances. Disturbances such as a CEO rejecting his bonus, or Bill Gates calling for creative capitalism, have only a small chance of spreading across the system. But this system is "fragile" in the sense that every so often, an event, which need not be of tremendous magnitude, will percolate widely across it.

Our understanding of how social norms and ethics evolve is highly imperfect. But in the real world norms and ethics are nonetheless of great practical importance. Mr. Gates's perception is that a change in attitude is needed among Western business leaders. He believes this would speed up economic development. It might. But it might also do the even more important work of securing allegiance to the sometimes embattled ideas of markets and capitalism, and to the political system of liberal democracy.

OLD-FASHIONED CAPITALISM IS MORAL ENOUGH

William Easterly

I am rather puzzled by Paul Ormerod's comment. I certainly agree that social norms and ethics affect everyone's behavior. For example, norms are quite effective in deterring cheating in business transactions because unsubtle cheating would disgrace or ostracize a businessman. But selling people a lot of things they want is not cheating or unethical, so I am not sure what Professor Ormerod thinks is wrong with the ethics of business.

And where exactly is the evidence that corporate philanthropy toward the poor has become enough of a social norm that it will make a huge difference both to the poor and to the image of capitalism? I think most people will be more convinced by the huge amount of evidence that conventional capitalism brings increased wages for unskilled workers than they will be impressed by creative capitalism because of a few pennies for AIDS victims from Product RED T-shirts sold by the Gap.

Falling all over ourselves apologizing for capitalism and

then offering a token amount of corporate philanthropy to repair its imagined defects is lame. If consumers want those corporations to give a little bit of the money to the poor, then I am sure corporations will respond to demand. But as a force against poverty, this is small beer, based on any available track record I know of. A more reliable path to success against poverty is simply to take advantage of all the power of conventional capitalism—a power that has been abundantly demonstrated by the steady fall of global poverty over the decades. (One of the triumphs of capitalism is that it overcomes the probability of failure in most human enterprises, which Professor Ormerod describes so well in his book *Why Most Things Fail*.)

As far as the fact that the Great Depression led some to favor Soviet planning—well, that was obviously a mistake, wasn't it! Hopefully, few will make the same mistake again by overreacting to the current financial crisis. The secret is to keep our eyes on the long run and not the short run. (Keynes's snide remark that we're all dead in the long run totally missed the point: first, we do see the payoff in our lifetime, and second, it's thanks to our parents' commitment to free markets that we are where we are. Shouldn't we do the same for our children?) In the long run the Chinese Communist Party dictatorship that Professor Ormerod sees as a rival gave us famines, great leaps backward, cultural revolutions, and deaths of tens of millions, and yes, the recent boom. But the latter came when the Communist mandarins gave up much of their totalitarian power to markets.

Yes, capitalism is frustratingly unstable and unequal. Financial crises recur time and again. But what other system comes close to delivering the kind of cornucopia that Professor Ormerod acknowledges? The twentieth-century economists who got it right in the long run were Joseph Schumpeter and Friedrich Hayek, who understood the gales of creative destruction and the chaos and unpredictability of free individuals interacting, yet realized that that very chaotic freedom was the nursery of a material abundance unlike anything the world had ever seen.

TO GATES'S CRITICS: YOU'RE MAKING PERFECT THE ENEMY OF THE GOOD

Elizabeth Stuart

Bill Easterly is right that more corporate social responsibility is not going to solve global poverty. But this is a straw man, and it shouldn't be used to dismiss what could be a great idea. A more useful reading of creative capitalism might involve just one part of the triumvirate that history suggests can lift people out of the misery of poverty. True creative capitalism would not be based in a company's PR department but would instead be central to its core business functions. Yes, it would bring either profit or recognition—and at best, both—but it would also mean innovation and new working relationships. It is the latter that presents the greatest opportunity for real change.

An example: When the private sector thinks about climate change, it usually centers on a carbon footprint strategy, a strategy that shows how emissions in headquarters and the field will be cut. But the true creative capitalists, having recognized that global warming threatens their business model just as it threatens progress in poor countries, would look for much more fundamental ways to engage with the issue. They would join with climate change activists in lobbying Congress. They would invest more in their supply chains, so that cotton farmers in Africa would still be able to grow their crops if weather patterns were to change significantly. And working with communities in poor countries, they would develop technologies such as cheap, solar-powered stoves—technologies that might also have applications in the rich world.

Drug companies' donating medicines to poor countries makes for nice publicity. But the practice is also potentially dangerous. If the firm needs to tighten its belt, that free antiretroviral program in Zambia or Lesotho is going to get scrapped, with dire results for the beneficiaries. However, a pharmaceutical company that works to improve poor people's access to drugs in the long term—by, for instance, taking drugs off patent as quickly as possible—is a true corporate philanthropist.

And while Professor Easterly thinks it too difficult to ask poor consumers what they want, entrepreneurs are successfully doing just that. Those at the bottom of the pyramid talk with their dollars, just like any other customer. In his book *India Unbound,* the former CEO of Procter & Gamble describes selling people in rural areas products they can actually afford, like washing powder in single-serve sachets.

This is not to say that innovation and new partnerships alone will be enough. If the corporate sector is going to be a genuine part of the solution, it will need to accept some unsavories: greater regulation and improved labor conditions. Easterly says that one of the ways capitalism helps people around the world is by employing them in their factories. Well, yes, but too many international companies reserve the well-paid jobs for foreigners and export most of their profits.

Two caveats. We need to be realistic: Development is going

to take time. It would be unthinkable to allow African countries to suffer for centuries in the way that preindustrialized Europe did, and we can probably transfer enough learning to help them skip some of the rungs on the development ladder. But there are few quick fixes, and much of what works will be time consuming and demoralizing. The implication of Easterly's argument, however, is that because progress has been slow and development experts have failed in the past, we should give up on philanthropic development. That just makes the perfect the enemy of the good.

THE PROBLEM WITH GATES: DO AS I SAY, NOT AS I DID

Clive Crook

When somebody says "Microsoft," my first thought is unlikely to be "good corporate citizen." I am more likely to think, "world-transforming innovator," "awesome creator of wealth," and "ruthless competitor." (Sorry, Bill, no disrespect.) One wonders what would have become of this company if in its first decade or two its founder had spent significant time and effort—as he urged his audience at Davos—on good works not directly related to his goals for the enterprise. So my main reaction to Bill's speech was that it was a comical instance of "Do as I say, not as I did." Microsoft's shareholders and the world at large can thank their lucky stars that Bill did not follow his own advice.

Because he was an old-fashioned uncreative capitalist for so long, Gates changed the world and accumulated the means to become a staggeringly generous—and notably creative—philanthropist. His and Melinda's remarkable charitable efforts are not a tax on Microsoft's financial or intellectual resources. They are outlays from their personal fortune. This is private, not corporate, philanthropy—a crucial distinction that Bill's speech rather obscures.

John D. Rockefeller's philosophy was to succeed in business as much as possible and by any means necessary, so that during his life and especially at the end of it he would have more to give away to good causes. I'm with Milton Friedman on this: Apart from anything else, I prefer the clarity of Rockefeller's approach. The principle of "corporate social responsibility" which Bill now wants to advance is convoluted and incoherent, in my view, and even if it were to amount to something, it's still a potentially debilitating distraction from the search for profit. Let businesses be businesses. Once wealth has been created and taxes paid, its owners can spend it on good works.

Yet even if they choose not to give, the world is still better off. Microsoft's contribution to global welfare is orders of magnitude larger than the outlays of the Gates Foundation and all the other charitable spending of the firm's employees and shareholders.

Microsoft is an extreme case because of its size and success, but it nonetheless represents a much wider phenomenon. The world's most successful enterprises make a habit of concentrating implacably on improving their products, growing their businesses, and destroying their rivals. It is a commonplace to point out, following Adam Smith, that although it may be the last thing on their minds, businessmen who dedicate themselves to this task advance our world's collective prosperity more than any other members of society. Now Bill tells us that this is not enough. Capitalism also needs to be creative. What can one say to this? Capitalism is creative, and nothing else comes close. Depending on just what meaning you append to this redundant expression, "creative capitalism" actually seems likely to be less creative than the kind we already have.

I'll come back to that in a moment. First, though, Mike Kinsley assures us that Bill "obviously" did not mean to say that capitalism-as-it-exists is not creative, just that it could be more creative. It was good to have that confirmed. The fact that it needed to be suggests that the term was not well chosen. In fact, Bill is not just saying that capitalism is great but can do even better, as Mike's clarification would have it. He appears to be saying that it fails systematically in one surpassingly important respect:

> *Why do people benefit in inverse proportion to their need? Market incentives make that happen.*
>
> *In a system of pure capitalism, as people's wealth rises, the financial incentive to serve them rises. As their wealth falls, the financial incentive to serve them falls—until it becomes zero.*

Under capitalism, people benefit in inverse proportion to their needs? Didn't Karl Marx say something like that? It happens to be nonsense: Capitalism has created mass affluence. As for there being no market incentive to serve the poor, tell it to Sam Walton. Yet this nexus of misconceptions is widely embraced. I would be amazed if Bill did not actually believe that free-enterprise capitalism is the best way to spread prosperity. In his speech, however, he affects to question it. He appeases, rather than confronts, the prejudices of those who not merely question capitalism but are certain that it is fundamentally evil. I think that is a cop-out, and it does the poor and economically excluded of this world no favors at all.

Rhetoric aside, what does Bill's "more creative capitalism" actually involve? Several things, it seems. One is effective philanthropy or, if you will, "creative philanthropy"—a much better label for what the Gates Foundation is about than "creative capitalism." The foundation has changed the way philanthropy works not just through scale but also by subjecting its endeavors to rigorous tests of efficiency and effectiveness. In other words, it is bringing the discipline of business to charitable works. This seems an obviously good thing, not to mention overdue. But it is really the opposite of what many people took Bill to mean in his speech. This is bringing business ideas to philanthropy, not bringing philanthropic ideas to business.

Indeed, if you are talking about ordinary public companies, there is a problem with bringing philanthropic ideas to doing business. Let's be clear about this. In the case of public companies, corporate philanthropy that neither is directed by shareholders nor intended to serve their interests is the next best thing to theft—as Warren Buffett, back when he was uncreative, used to note. Giving away other people's money may be charitable, but it is also unethical. In the modern corporation, executives often need reminding that they are employees rather than owners, and that their first duty is to shareholders. A preoccupation with corporate social responsibility helps them to forget.

Of course, "creative capitalism" could indeed refer to philanthropy that does serve shareholders' interests—for instance, by improving the firm's image with customers or by making it easier and cheaper to recruit and retain the best employees. Sometimes social investments turn out to be profitable businesses, too: One thinks of microfinance. Call me a cynic, but eventually there might be some money in Gates's plan to develop "a text-free interface that will enable illiterate or semiliterate people to use a PC instantly, with minimal training or assistance." (And just so I am not misunderstood, its profit potential does not lead me to oppose the idea.) Initial philanthropic outlays in cases like these are really just another kind of business investment.

If opportunities of this sort to make money are being missed, bring on creative capitalists to uncover and exploit them. However, this is not a new kind of capitalism or some economic "third way" that requires a new way of thinking about business. This is the old way of thinking about business. And I am fine with that: It is Bill who is arguing that the old way will no longer do.

Let me close for the moment by noting another moment in the speech that made my spirits sink: "I hope that the great thinkers here [in Davos] will dedicate some time to finding ways for businesses, governments, NGOs, and the media to create measures of what companies are doing to use their power and intelligence to serve a wider circle of people. This kind of information is an important element of creative capitalism. It can turn good works into recognition, and ensure that recognition brings market-based rewards to businesses that do the most work to serve the most people."

Gates believes it is possible to make comparisons—to say that some firms are doing better than others and thus deserve more "recognition"—and this in turn requires valuations of some kind. But these things are apples and oranges. Not even the greatest minds are going to be able to make the incommensurable add up. Moreover, the idea seems to envisage collaboration among businesses, governments, NGOs, and the media, of all things, in coming up with standardized measures of social enterprise. And if you can measure it, you can regulate it. I wonder what the old (I mean young) Bill Gates would have thought of that.

THE PROBLEM WITH FRIEDMAN: A LACK OF IMAGINATION

Brad DeLong

All this talk about Milton Friedman's 1970 essay "The Social Responsibility of Business" gives me an opportunity to get something off my chest that has been lying there for decades: Friedman's argument has never made any sense to me.

Of corporate social responsibility, Friedman writes that

> the corporate executive would be spending someone else's money for a general social interest. Insofar as his actions in accord with his social responsibility reduce returns to stockholders, he is spending their money. Insofar as his actions raise the price to customers, he is spending the customers' money. Insofar as his actions lower the wages of some employees, he is spending their money.

The stockholders or the customers or the employees could separately spend their own money on the particular action if they wished to do so. The executive is exercising a distinct "social responsibility," rather than serving as an agent of the stockholders or the customers or the employees, only if he spends the money in a different way than they would have spent it.

But if he does this, he is in effect imposing taxes, on the one hand, and deciding how the tax proceeds shall be spent, on the other.

This is weak toast. This is thoroughly unconvincing. What reason is there not to turn this around? What reason is there not to say, instead:

• If customers don't want to pay higher prices and so buy from corporations that pursue social responsibility, they are (as long as product markets are competitive) free to do so at their leisure.

• If workers don't want to receive lower wages by working for corporations that pursue social responsibility, they are (as long as labor markets are competitive) free to do so at their leisure.

• If investors don't want to receive lower profits by investing in corporations that pursue social responsibility, they are (as long as capital markets are competitive) free to do so at their leisure.

If workers, customers, and investors expect that the executives of the corporations they deal with will pursue social responsibility objectives, where's the foul? The executives aren't doing anything wrong at any level—they are in fact performing a valuable function: They are being the trusted and honest agents of the workers, consumers, and investors by pursuing social responsibility goals. They are helping them pool their resources to achieve what they want to see happen. This pooling-of-resources agency function is an important one—it is, after all, why we have large organizations in the first place. So why limit it to narrowly profit-maximizing goals?

Friedman never gives us an answer.

WHERE'S THE HARM?

Clive Crook

Since I just declared myself a Friedmanite on corporate social responsibility, I owe Brad a prompt reply to his post in which he says Friedman got it all wrong. Where's the foul, asks Brad, if a company dedicates itself to good works as well as making money—and its workers, customers, and investors are aware of that and happy with it?

I don't know what Friedman would have said to that, but my reply is no foul—in the sense that nobody is being cheated. There would also be no foul, in that same sense, if a company said it intended to dedicate itself exclusively to good works and had no intention of making any money at all—again, so long as everybody, including investors, was content with this. For that matter, there also would be no foul if a company said it would dedicate itself to making its workers miserable, asking its customers to pay double what they needed to, and bilking investors of every last cent—no foul, as before, so long as all interested parties were in the picture and thought it was fine. Caveat emptor, by all means.

The question is not "Where's the foul?" It's "Where's the harm?" What counts is which of this potentially limitless set of no-foul organizing principles is likely to produce the best results. Friedman believed that the profit motive was hugely underrated as an organizing principle that can produce socially beneficial results. In my view, he was surely right about that. Ordinary profit-seeking capitalism gets terrible press. Even capitalists who have done as much as Bill Gates to advance social welfare aren't willing to defend it. And this is where corporate social responsibility comes in. It is a response, in substantial part, to a widely held misconception about the profit motive. I think that Friedman mainly wanted to correct the misconception and draw attention to the unintended consequences of adopting organizing principles different from, and supposedly more enlightened than, the profit motive.

Would the wide adoption of a broader corporate goal than seeking profits really make us better off? As I argued in my previous post, if Gates had been a CSR enthusiast right from the start, I doubt that there would ever have been a Microsoft or a Gates Foundation.

TO CAPITALISM'S DEFENDERS: DON'T BE SO DEFENSIVE

Matthew Bishop

Why do defenders of the profit maximization orthodoxy instinctively recoil at the idea of creative capitalism? One very good reason, as Easterly's response to Paul Ormerod reflects, is a fear that applauding these strategies implies a criticism of capitalism and gives ground to those pushing other economic systems (like state planning). This is a legitimate concern—capitalism is the best system we have to meet the needs of the people on this planet—but maybe we should be more confident. And a bit more realistic.

Let's assume for now that we all agree with Richard Posner's claim, backed by Clive Crook and others, that "corporate managers have a fiduciary duty to maximize corporate profits." The problem is that they mostly don't.

Despite twenty-five years in which shareholders have increasingly championed profit maximization, firms often seem to fall short of that goal. Even the firms that have been persuaded to embrace this goal by shareholders often fail to deliver, not least by confusing unsustainable short-term increases in profitability with long-term profit maximization. Why is this?

The success—measured by a soaring share price—of creatively capitalistic firms such as Google or Salesforce, both of which give away 1 percent of their equity, profits, and employees' time under a "1 percent rule," suggests that pursuing social good can be rewarded by the market. In these cases, it can be argued that shareholders are rewarding their social mission, although it almost certainly costs them profit in the short run, because these owners calculate that the returns from PR charity and jump-start charity (in Posner's elegant taxonomy) exceed the costs. Or perhaps, as Gates suggests, they see the valuable impact that being a mission-driven creative capitalist has on their reputation or staff recruitment and productivity.

But if creative capitalism can be so profitable, why are there so few examples? Moreover, if investing in social responsibility can be good for shareholders, why are defenders of profit-maximizing capitalism so reluctant to praise corporate programs aimed at helping society?

There is certainly a long list of firms that have sacrificed profitability by failing to invest in corporate citizenship early enough—most famously, Shell, Nike, and Nestlé have each lost market share through damage to their reputations and have had to invest heavily to claw back up. Yet if they had focused on investing significant resources in their social strategy sooner, would the defenders of the profit maximization orthodoxy have been supporters or critics?

A lot of CSR activity may be wasteful, but as the old marketing saw goes: "I know that half of my advertising budget is a waste of money, I just don't know which half." Large corporations work in a complex global marketplace, where they face enormous uncertainty; creative capitalism is about a response to that uncertainty. The challenge for this debate is to identify what works and what does not, not to count angels dancing on the head of the profit maximization pin.

One reason why the defenders of capitalism seem not to want it to "go creative" is their assumption that there should be some clear division of labor between corporations and government. This is eloquently put in Milton Friedman's article, using two arguments:

1. "I share Adam Smith's skepticism about the benefits that can be expected from 'those who affected to trade for the public good.'"

2. Corporations pushing social objectives other than profit maximization "are seeking to attain by undemocratic procedures what they cannot attain by democratic procedures."

Taking the second point first: There is a tacit assumption here about the efficiency of democratic procedures. But if these procedures are failing, as many contributors agree is the case in developing countries, then can we assume that corporations ought to stay away from "public good" issues? They may be a second best solution, but why make unattainable perfection the enemy of the good?

Posner anticipates this argument, claiming that "charity" simply reduces the pressure for reform in developing countries. Yet this is not an argument from first principle, like Friedman's, but an empirical point. Perhaps some palliative "opiate of the people" charity that eases the frustrations of the public would have the unfortunate effect that Posner anticipates. Yet maybe done well, it will actually move society toward better governance. As Glaeser points out, investing in building strong private institutions and educating the workforce can be revolutionary acts.

This takes us to Friedman's first point—in support of which he doesn't really introduce evidence—that businesses getting involved in social issues won't achieve very much. Posner, like Friedman, is right to question the outcomes here: Much CSR is cosmetic and not focused on impact. He is also right that competition drives corporations to be efficient. Yet this is a challenge to creative capitalism, not a refutation of it. Advocates of creative capitalism need to be transparent about what they are doing and compete for shareholder approval on the grounds that their social investments are long-run profit-maximizing examples of enlightened self-interest. Shareholders should certainly ask hard questions about whether these investments are really using the assets of the firm most effectively to manage risk and uncertainty. But they should do so in the same spirit with which they analyze the firm's investments in research and development or global expansion. That way creative capitalism might fulfill its potential.

A Response to Elizabeth Stuart:
IF NOT PROFITS, WHAT?
William Easterly

I am not clear what Elizabeth Stuart thinks is going to motivate corporations in her new paradigm if it is not profits. What is going to drive the "innovation and new working relationships" and new "core business functions"? On what basis will corporations choose functions and relationships that are not profit oriented, and where will they find the equity investors and lenders to fund such efforts? If they are not guided by the market, how will firms decide what to produce and for whom?

Sometimes I do get what Ms. Stuart seems to be implying, which is that corporations are overlooking their own self-interest viewed in traditional profit terms. I grant that markets are not perfect and there could be such cases, like maybe the opportunities to sell solar-powered stoves or washing powder in single-serve sachets, or to offer deep discounts on drugs to the poor (price discrimination is an established way of doing business). This is the view represented most famously in C. K. Prahalad's *The Fortune at the Bottom of the Pyramid.* There is something to this insight, but there is also much that it overlooks. A formidable barrier to selling to the poor is that revenues per transaction are small, and if transaction costs are high, then it is simply not worth the trouble. Corporations are not as dumb as the bottom-of-the-pyramid promoters think they are.

Other times Ms. Stuart seems to conflate public and private goods. The environment is a public good, and addressing climate change requires public action. Corporations have no private incentive to fix climate problems (although they might be very entrepreneurial if public action "such as a carbon tax" created some private incentive to find new climate-friendly technologies).

As far as finding rapid growth, I never said give up. I said we "experts" don't know how to achieve it, and false "expert knowledge" makes rapid growth less likely. There is progress against poverty, but it is mostly gradual rather than rapid. Yes, some countries have found rapid growth—East Asian tigers, mainly—but so far they are rare exceptions. I sympathize with a quest for such success. Big-time success in the business world is also rare, but businessmen still keep trying for big-time success! The odds against finding rapid escapes from poverty are great, but if we beat the odds, the payoff is even greater. That's the beauty of capitalism.

WHY NOT EXPERIMENT?

Paul Ormerod

Professor Easterly is disarmingly flattering about my work, so it is not easy to take issue with him. And, in fact, we do agree on the fundamentals.

Two points put this beyond doubt. First, I consider myself an unequivocal enthusiast for both capitalism and liberal democracy. Second, like Professor Easterly, I regard Hayek as being by some margin the greatest social scientist of the twentieth century. The research agenda for the twenty-first century is dominated by his insights.

But capitalism is not the same as unrestrained free markets, mediated neither by formal regulation nor by informal norms. And a key insight of Hayek is that we make progress not by the "rational" analysis of the central planner but by experiment and evolution. I think this is how we should see Mr. Gates's suggestion—as an experiment. It is an idea that is intended to bring benefits. Like most things, it is likely to fail. But until it is tried we will not know.

The Hayekian view of the world is completely at odds with the argument that we should never do anything to interfere with the Platonic ideal of the Market found in economic theory. We experiment and see what works. Capitalism comes in different forms. Yes, America is the most successful, but the pinko Europeans in Germany, France, and Sweden—each with its own particular variant of capitalism—have not done too badly either.

Like it or not, the behavior of many financial and commercial companies in recent years has damaged the image of capitalism. Many executives have collected massive rewards for failure at no personal risk to themselves. Outside America, even in the liberal democracies of Western Europe, there is still a reservoir of hostility to capitalism. This needs to be dispelled at every opportunity.

And yes, Professor Easterly, I am skeptical about a lot of what goes on under the heading of corporate social responsibility. I am particularly wary of the central-planning mentality that often goes with it: the belief that sufficient data and sufficient research will enable us to guarantee the success of a particular measure—the triumph of hope over the experience of ages. But the Hayekian process of evolution will eventually find this hope to be insufficient. We've known since Adam Smith that we do not have to intend good in order to achieve good. But in the meantime we might, just occasionally, want to intend good.

CAPITALISM WORKS BECAUSE IT'S SELF-CORRECTING

William Easterly

Professor Ormerod, in your last post, I thought you were feeding stereotypes of evil corporate leaders more than you were analyzing the capitalist system. With defenses of capitalism like this, I don't think we're going to have much success "dispelling hostility to capitalism."

When you write that "the behavior of many financial and commercial companies in recent years has damaged the image of capitalism. Many executives have collected massive rewards for failure at no personal risk to themselves," I think you are extrapolating from a few well-publicized bad apples to a sweeping claim that is not supported by evidence or common sense. Could any market systematically and persistently reward failure and consistently insulate decision makers from the consequences of failure without quickly exhausting its investment capital? I doubt it. Sure, there can be crises like the current one, in which a lot of investments go bad, but most of the investors are indeed suffering and are frantically seeking better investment havens (and quickly jettisoning the managers who failed and looking for those who will produce success).

Capitalism does indeed have very bad times, and it goes off the rails temporarily. But it is self-correcting, which is why the rails lead so steadily upward and onward. The big story about liberal democratic capitalism is the tremendous material abundance that it has produced wherever it exists. The defining story of the last few decades is not the crisis of 2007–2008 but the biggest mass escape from poverty in human history from 1960 onward.

Why are we so quick to lose sight of the big picture because of a few bad guys who got away with fraud and irresponsible risk taking? The evil CEO is a visceral bogeyman invoked by those who fear and hate the liberal economic order. But have even the worst CEOs in the history of capitalism committed crimes on the same order as the worst decision makers in other human systems, like the worst political leaders of the last century? Or the worst religious leaders, from the Inquisition to today's terrorism? I'll take my chances with democratic capitalism, even if a few horrible managers get perverse rewards every once in a while. It may make us awfully boring, but economists are right to emphasize statistical trends and overall capitalist performance over temporary panics, anecdotes, and Hollywood stereotypes about evil CEOs.

PURE VERSUS CREATIVE CAPITALISM: A FALSE CHOICE

Ed Glaeser

I think it is a terrible mistake to frame creative capitalism as an alternative to capitalism and to justify creative capitalism as a response to the failings of the free market. Professor Easterly is surely correct to suggest that standard capitalism has and will be an enormously powerful force for improving the lives of the world's poorest citizens. He is also correct to suggest that creative capitalism is likely to be a niche sector that appeals to a modest number of workers or investors. But that doesn't mean creative capitalism is a bad idea.

If there are wealthy philanthropists who seek an alternative to traditional giving, and if there are altruistic workers who want to combine a decent income with some charitable activities, then surely it is reasonable to consider alternative contractual forms that might cater to these desires. Thinking about alternative contractual forms does not imply that there is anything wrong with either the existing for-profit or not-for-profit sectors. Nor does it imply that hybrid contractual forms will solve all the world's problems.

Framing this debate as procapitalists against anticapitalists will lead us down the wrong path. The right question is whether our current laws allow enough organizational innovation. And I can't see why the enemies of creative capitalism are so confident about the legal status quo.

WHAT ARE WE TALKING ABOUT?

Steven Landsburg

It would help a lot, I think, if we could agree on what we're talking about. So let me try to pin down what creative capitalism (CC) is. More precisely, let me try to pin down how a CC firm differs from the firms we meet in economics textbooks.

In the textbook firm, all the revenue goes to workers and investors. At the CC firm, some revenue goes to something else. Where does that revenue come from? The laws of arithmetic admit only four possibilities:

A. It comes from the workers.
B. It comes from the investors.
C. It comes from the consumers.
D. It comes from nobody, because the CC firm can use labor and capital more efficiently than the textbook firm.

It is quite impossible to have a sensible discussion about the prospects for creative capitalism without specifying which of the four possibilities we have in mind. (Of course, we are free to consider all the possibilities in turn.)

Once we specify an assumption, we can draw some conclusions.

By way of illustration, consider assumption A: The workers at the CC firm accept lower wages, presumably because they like knowing that they're working at a CC firm. Instead of being paid, say, $10 an hour, the worker gets $8 an hour and $2 goes to some worthy cause. From the firm's point of view, labor still costs $10 an hour, so the capital-labor ratio, the return to investors, the value of the company stock, et cetera, is all the same as at the textbook firm. The advent of CC firms increases the supply of labor (perhaps only slightly) and hence drives down both economy-wide wages and the economy-wide capital-labor ratio (again, perhaps only slightly).

Assumptions B, C, and D each yields other conclusions. Those conclusions might depend on auxiliary assumptions about preferences. In case D, some auxiliary assumptions are definitely needed to explain where the added efficiency comes from (maybe the gratification of working at a CC firm makes workers more energetic?).

But any meaningful discussion of what CC will lead to depends on specifying whether we're in world A, B, C, or D (or some combination) and what the auxiliary assumptions are. If we're not concrete about that, all we can do is talk past each other. If we are concrete about that, we can settle most of our disagreements with a little bit of math. (Although we'll then have to deal with the disagreements about which assumptions are most plausible.)

All four varieties of CC may well be worthy of discussion, and surely all four discussions can go on simultaneously. But insofar as specific assertions are made, it would be good to be clear which of the four varieties (and, if relevant, which subvarieties) they're meant to apply to.

IN DEFENSE OF A GOOD REPUTATION

Michael Kremer

According to Bill Gates, companies should be motivated to serve the poor not just by financial rewards but by recognition. Most of those who have responded have argued strongly against this idea: They maintain that a corporation's duty is to serve the financial interests of its shareholders, and anything else risks undermining the capitalist system that has created our prosperity. These critics take the position that it is more efficient for business to make money and let governments and philanthropists handle the problem of how to redistribute it.

I agree that the main duty of a CEO is to his or her shareholders, and I have no illusions that creative capitalism can replace government redistribution. Businesses are and should be primarily concerned with getting returns for their shareholders, and the government should handle questions of redistribution. That said, I disagree with Milton Friedman's absolutist position. In some limited situations, businesses are able to redistribute more efficiently than governments are.

Because this is true, it is difficult to make an argument against corporate social responsibility or creative capitalism based solely on concerns about efficiency. The argument against creative capitalism has to be a more complicated one—perhaps an argument about how changing corporate goals will lead to a slippery slope or undermine the legitimacy of capitalism. But those arguments would lead to a very different kind of conversation.

There are several reasons why it might be more efficient for companies, rather than the government, to redistribute. First, many companies have some market power—that is, the firm controls enough of the market for a particular good that it can raise prices without losing all its customers. By the same logic, if the firm slightly lowers the price, the loss in profits the firm will suffer will be very small. But the gain in social welfare may be substantial.

Gregory Clark and Gary Becker suggest that firms in competitive industries cannot engage in altruism or they would go out of business, but I'm skeptical. Clark cites the airline industry as an example, so let's go with that. From a strictly profit-maximizing perspective, there is some optimal number of routes Lufthansa should supply. Suppose Lufthansa found that it lost $15,000 last year on a particular African route. But the social benefits of bringing more tourists and businesspeople to Africa—and bringing down airfares for Africans traveling out of the continent—would almost certainly exceed $15,000. I wouldn't condemn the directors of Lufthansa if they decided to keep flying the route, and I doubt it would drive them out of business.

To take another airline example, consider the issue of whether Virgin Atlantic Airways should cover antiretroviral treatment for employees in South Africa. Let's suppose that the labor market in South Africa is such that Virgin Atlantic Airways could easily attract a very good staff with a health insurance plan that does not cover antiretroviral treatment. Would it be wise for Virgin Atlantic to design such a compensation package? It seems likely that any benefit from doing so would be outweighed by the damage to Virgin's brand name. Consumers may not choose Virgin on account of the company's altruism, but they may well choose it based on overall brand image, of which altruism is a part. And it wouldn't take many of these consumers to make providing the antiretroviral treatment a wise business decision.

One of the most interesting points in Gates's talk was his claim that an altruistic reputation may help a firm recruit talented employees. Some of the economists in this discussion seem to take the position that potential employees care primarily about money, and relegate altruistic motives to a footnote. But an alternate view is that what people really care about is status, and there are plenty of ways to achieve status besides money. Indeed, what produces status is something society can shape. The awards given to professionals in advertising, journalism, academia, the entertainment industry, and the military are all proof.

There is good reason to think that employees value nonpecuniary factors when choosing employers. Scott Stern of Northwestern, for example, has shown that employees are willing to accept relatively large pay cuts to take positions in the biopharmaceutical industry that allow them to continue publishing. Many graduating lawyers seek firms that do pro bono work. And many in the IT sector want to work for companies that are seen as cool and cutting edge.

Indeed, it's a little ironic that creative capitalism has been proposed by someone often seen as a symbol of profit-maximizing capitalism, and so many of his biggest critics here are academics and journalists—professionals for whom the primary form of reward is recognition.

Once we accept that some customers, employees, and regulators are motivated by desires other than profit maximization, then we can easily imagine that some companies have opportunities to transfer a dollar to the poor at a cost of much less than a dollar to their shareholders. And it presumably costs government considerably more to redistribute dollars, since there are administrative costs and behavior-distorting inefficiencies associated with taxation.

WHAT ARE WE TALKING ABOUT? PART TWO

Steven Landsburg

By way of harping on the point I made before, let me point to a paragraph from Michael Kremer's post here:

Suppose Lufthansa found that it lost $15,000 last year on a particular African route. But the social benefits of bringing more tourists and businesspeople to Africa—and bringing down airfares for Africans traveling out of the continent—would almost certainly exceed $15,000. I wouldn't condemn the directors of Lufthansa if they decided to keep flying the route, and I doubt it would drive them out of business.

I too doubt that this would drive Lufthansa out of business. But that does not absolve us from thinking about where the $15,000 comes from.

Vision 1: Investors accept a below-market rate of return in exchange for the privilege of supporting Lufthansa's good works. This raises the question (raised many times in many other posts) of why investors would not prefer to earn higher returns and make their own charitable contributions. Insofar as the answer depends on tax consequences, we have the implication that the desired level of creative capitalism should vary substantially with changes in the tax code.

Vision 2: Investors won't accept a below-market rate of return, and therefore Lufthansa's stock price drops. Lufthansa now has less capital to work with, rendering Lufthansa's employees less productive than other airlines'.

Visions 3 and 4: Lufthansa employees accept lower wages, or Lufthansa passengers pay higher prices, in exchange for the privilege of supporting Lufthansa's good works. In this case, Lufthansa can still be profit maximizing (just like a company that keeps its employees happy by providing them with a gym or keeps its customers happy by putting a prize in every box of Cracker Jack). Profit-maximizing creative capitalism is going to look very different from non-profit-maximizing creative capitalism, and we should think about how.

Vision 5: Lufthansa's employees are so energized by Lufthansa's good works that they are more productive throughout the day. Once again, this looks like profit maximization.

Several previous posters have explicitly elaborated on one or more of these visions. I think we need more of that kind of precision. If we don't supply that, we're not doing our jobs.

CREATIVE CAPITALISM HAS ITS FIRST TOOL

Loretta Michaels

The debate here tends to assume that the world is divided into two camps: the nonprofit, charitable sector with its focus on "good" causes and the for-profit, free-market-driven world of business with its focus on, well, profits. Firmly supporting this bipolar division are the many rules and regulations governing what foundations, private investors, pension and endowment funds, and other pools of funds may do with their money. As a result charities are scrambling for limited funds, while there are large quantities of market-driven wealth that are prohibited from socially responsible investing because the return on that investment is inadequate. And sitting in the middle are lots of worthy causes that are capable of being self-sufficient; they just don't offer enough of a return to attract for-profit investors.

A new Vermont law seeks to address this issue by creating what is essentially a charity hybrid: a tax-exempt entity that is able to attract and generate private capital for its initiatives. The low-profit, limited liability corporation (or L3C) seeks to combine the features of a regular limited liability company with the socially beneficial aspects of a nonprofit. The goal is to create a way to make charities self-sufficient, rather than having to rely on donated funds to stay afloat.

A key element of these hybrids is the Program Related Investment, an IRS-sanctioned investment that a foundation can make in a for-profit business venture to support a charitable activity. While such investments are allowed to generate income and appreciate in value, that cannot be the intended outcome. So a foundation can invest funds and have them count as a grant for tax purposes, but it can do so in areas that would not normally be open to charitable investing because the risk/return profile would be considered too jeopardizing.

But until now these investments haven't been widely used because there hasn't been a clearly defined vehicle for receiving them. Foundations interested in making such investments have had to appeal to the IRS on an individual basis, which can take years and cost thousands of dollars. But the L3C is structured in such a way that it automatically complies with IRS regulations, so interested foundations no longer have to go through the rigmarole of seeking IRS approval.

What this means in practice is that a private organization operating as an L3C can seek out investments from several types of investors and allocate risk and reward accordingly—with foundations assuming higher risk and lower rates of return. So private capital could invest in separate layers of funding that guarantee market rates of return, thus opening the door to vast amounts of money, such as pension funds, which are currently unavailable for socially beneficial purposes. And of course there also can be a middle ground for investors willing to invest at lower rates of return for philanthropic reasons, like a bank wishing to fulfill its community reinvestment requirements.

The potential for the L3C is enormous, and the new Vermont law is generating a great deal of interest. The ability to bring together foundations, private investors, nonprofits and for-profit entities, all with their different risk requirements, to achieve common goals will pave the way for many worthy causes that would otherwise languish. Instead of endlessly debating whether government, charity, or industry should be solving a particular problem, interested parties and stakeholders can design solutions that meet everyone's needs.

WHY ISN'T REGULAR CAPITALISM GOOD ENOUGH?

Steven Landsburg

Lifting large populations out of poverty is the noblest cause I can imagine, and I'm glad Bill Gates is thinking about how to do it. I want to think about it too. A good way to start is to ask what's worked in the past. As far as I'm aware, there's only one answer: In every historical instance, substantial progress against poverty has been a side effect of general economic growth. Nothing else has ever worked. That's not an ideological statement; it's a fact.

Growth, in turn, is fostered most effectively by capitalism and policies that promote capitalism: low taxes, well-enforced property rights, functioning markets, and free trade. The primary cause of poverty is insufficient capitalism.

But there are two problems with using capitalism to fight poverty: First, there's a lot of entrenched resistance to capitalism, say, among corrupt third-world dictators. Second, capitalism takes time to work. I feel reasonably confident that the single best strategy for fighting tropical diseases over the next fifteen years would be to turn sub-Saharan Africa into a free trade zone. But if your child has just contracted malaria, you might not want to wait fifteen years.

So it is entirely right and proper to think hard about what Bill Gates calls creative capitalism and to applaud his commitment to this cause. It's also important to get the details right.

For example: Bill applauds the recent legislation that rewards drug companies for breakthroughs against neglected diseases with expedited FDA review for another of their products. The concept is wonderful; how it would be carried out seems nuts. Priority review is worth anywhere from zero to several hundred million dollars depending on what other product you've got in the pipeline. Why should the reward for fighting malaria be tied in such a bizarre way to whatever else you happen to be working on?

A far better way to carry out the idea would be to auction off the right to a priority review and set aside the auction proceeds as a reward for neglected-disease treatments. Now every firm faces the same hundreds-of-millions-of-dollars incentive. As a side benefit, the expedited review goes to the drug that is most likely to be a blockbuster, as well it should.

The underlying mistake here is to create an unnecessary link between the *funding* of a project and the project itself. The project is to reward a malaria treatment. The funds can come from anywhere. We might as well raise the funds in a way that makes sense. In fact, this method of fund-raising makes so much sense that it ought to be used whether or not the funds are earmarked for malaria research.

The RED program makes me uncomfortable for much the same reason. If I want to buy a watch and contribute to AIDS research, why can't I do those things separately, without buying a special RED watch? If the watchmaker wants to encourage my philanthropy, why not sell me an ordinary watch and urge me to contribute? Why are my consumption habits and my philanthropic habits being unnecessarily linked together?

Is there any psychological evidence that such linkage encourages more giving? Maybe, but I'm unaware of it. I hope someone has investigated this, and if so, I hope someone educates me.

Creative capitalism is good. Forced creativity in the form of unnecessary linkages (expedited review—malaria research, or watch buying–philanthropy) is suspect.

I realize that Bill Gates has done pretty well by bundling things that others might have preferred to keep separate. But I'd like to see the principle applied a little more judiciously.

YOU CAN MAKE PROFITS AND SAVE THE POOR

Michael Kremer

Actually, there is a way to harness the creativity of the capitalist system to address the needs of the poor that is consistent with letting businesses pursue profit maximization. The trick is to shape the incentives so that when firms pursue profits, they also address the needs of developing countries. Consider pharmaceutical firms' incentives to invest in R&D for drugs and vaccines for diseases that affect primarily developing countries—incentives that are, for parasitic diseases like schistosomiasis or leishmaniasis, quite limited. One study found that out of more than twelve hundred drugs developed between 1975 and 1997, only thirteen were for tropical diseases that hit the developing world hardest. And most of those thirteen were either developed by the military or were spillovers from products originally developed for veterinary purposes.

Incentives to develop products that treat tropical diseases are low not just because these diseases primarily affect the impoverished, but because of a variety of market and government failures. First, a market failure: People who take vaccines protect both themselves and others by breaking the cycle of disease transmission. But because they consider only their individual benefit when deciding whether or not take a vaccine, they will not be willing to pay a price that reflects the vaccine's full social benefit.

Then there is governmental failure: Once firms have undertaken costly and risky R&D on vaccines, governments have an incentive to use their market power to purchase the vaccine as cheaply as possible. Research on diseases like malaria, which affect many small developing countries, is thus subject to a free-rider problem: Because each individual country has an incentive to manipulate regulatory policy and intellectual property rights to obtain as low a price as possible, the pharmaceutical companies have little incentive to develop the much-needed drugs.

(These market and governmental failures also provide the answer to Gregory Clark's question about why we shouldn't simply give citizens of developing countries money and let them choose what they want to spend it on. In general, I am pretty sympathetic to the idea of providing cash grants to the poor, but in the case of genuine global public goods, like research on a malaria vaccine, cash transfers to individuals or even countries will not produce the desired outcome.)

In his Davos speech, Bill Gates mentioned one way to encourage pharmaceutical firms to invest in drugs and vaccines that address diseases of poor countries: under a recently instituted U.S. program, biopharmaceutical firms that develop products needed for poor countries are entitled to expedited regulatory review of other products by the FDA. Michael Kinsley and others have raised valid questions about this program. But there are other ways to encourage investment that would not be subject to the same criticism.

One possibility is advance market commitments (AMCs). Under AMCs, one or more sponsors (usually governments or private foundations) legally commit themselves to help finance purchases of a needed product, such as a malaria vaccine, once it is developed. In exchange, the developers who receive these funds agree to cap the long-run price of the product. And if no suitable product is developed, no AMC payments are made. A number of governments, along with the Gates Foundation, recently committed $1.5 billion to set up a pilot AMC program to develop a vaccine for pneumococcus, a pathogen that kills 1.6 million people each year, including almost 1 million children.

It's worth noting that advance market commitments not only help create incentives to develop new vaccines; they also help ensure access to vaccines for the people who need them most. They thus help avoid the conflict between innovation and access that too often dominates the debate over pharmaceuticals in the developing world. And by using advance market commitments, governments do not have to get involved in nettlesome decisions about which technological approaches are most promising—or, indeed, whether it's technically feasible to produce a product at all. The government simply says how much society is willing to pay for a vaccine and then sits back while the private sector competes to produce it.

One important difference between advance market commitments and the expedited review program Gates mentioned is that AMCs reward firms for the actual adoption and use of a product. This provides incentives for companies to focus their R&D efforts on products that would definitely be used, rather than on products that fit a set of technical specifications but are hard to apply to the real world.

There are, for example, many different technological approaches to developing a malaria vaccine. Some might provide only short-run protection, which would be useful to the military and travelers, who would make up a large share of the commercial market for a vaccine. And some might provide long-run protection, which would be better suited to protecting the 1 million people who die of malaria each year in developing countries. By linking the rewards to the product, AMCs would help ensure that the second kind of vaccine gets developed. And it would do so in an incredibly cost-effective fashion.

The health needs of the developed world are met by a combination of up-front public sector support for R&D and private sector research stimulated by the prospect of market profits. That same combination is needed to encourage R&D on the health needs of the poor as well. Recent years have seen considerable increases in "push" funding for R&D, but the "pull" of a market is still lacking. Advance market commitments could help provide that pull, bringing the creativity of capitalism to bear on the health problems of some of the world's poorest people.

CREATIVE CAPITALISM IS NOT PHILANTHROPY

Thierry Lefebvre

In this discussion the term "creative capitalism" has been seamlessly replaced by the likes of "corporate social responsibility," "corporate altruism," "corporate charity," and "corporate philanthropy." But I see nothing to suggest such equivalence in Gates's speech.

Of course, Mr. Gates's term is hazy, and so it is not surprising that the terms have cropped up and been interposed. But I do not blame him for the haziness. Some initial haziness—or room for improvement—can be important to stimulate discussion and bring forward ideas; haziness can be a marketing strategy.

In my view, Mr. Gates's notion is compatible with capitalism; in fact, it builds upon the very strength of the system.

Let's consider an example from Mr. Gates's speech: "I hope corporations will consider dedicating a percentage of your top innovators' time to issues that could help people left out of the global economy." The gut reaction of a well-behaved economist to this would be something along the lines of: (a) time is money; this is just another donation; (b) were it profitable to do so, people would already be doing it. These two conceptions are not necessarily true, however.

Take the first: In the course of a company's activity, people are not working 100 percent all the time. Sometimes they're up to 150 percent, and sometimes more around 70 percent. Nothing wrong with that; a business needs to be flexible and cannot be in full capacity all the time. However, to keep people involved in and excited about their jobs, it can make sense to give them pet projects devoted to using their skills in creative new ways when they have some free time. I think Mr. Gates is correct in thinking that focusing these projects on "philanthropic" activities is an efficient motivational tool for the "real" job as well.

For the second: Coordination in the efforts of companies might turn a nonprofitable market into a profitable one by stabilizing it. For instance, it could make perfect sense for corporations to subsidize life-prolonging medication if, as a result, the markets available to them become bigger and more stable. Disease, among its tragic consequences, is a source of uncertainty.

JUST DO THE RIGHT KIND OF LOBBYING

John Williamson

I agree with many of the criticisms that have been directed at Bill Gates's speech. "Creative capitalism" is essentially a new expression for what has long gone under the banner of corporate social responsibility. Many of the suggested practices are ways of maximizing profits, and enlightened self-interest may in fact be more profitable than going red in tooth and claw. But this hardly amounts to a novel theoretical insight. It is probably true that Bill Gates did more for the poor in his work as a businessman than he can hope to accomplish in his new role. One may not feel that maximizing the wealth of a shareholder is the most noble human calling, but firms that stray too far will get taken over by the more ruthless.

To avoid this fate, one has to go down Ed Glaeser's road and modify the contractual obligations of the firm. But while it would be nice to allow shareholders to modify the objectives of their firm so that anyone who took it over would still be subject to the same rules and would not be allowed to profit by sacrificing other social objectives, such a change demands government legislation, not an initiative by businessmen. If one wishes to increase the weight that business places on the needs of poor people, then the most natural, and probably most efficient, way of doing it is the boring traditional way of raising taxes on the rich in order to spend more on the poor.

At the same time, there seem to me to be important possibilities for the doctrine of corporate social responsibility—so derided by the critics—that have been overlooked in the discussion thus far: a firm's ability to change policies when the threat of takeover is minimal and to lobby for a change in the law when it is not.

Imagine a firm that is faced with a decision that could increase its profits but at the expense of some other social objective that most people consider important—the income of the poor, the preservation of a decent environment, the maintenance of healthy working conditions, energy economy, or whatever. There are two possibilities: Either the profit sacrifice is so marginal that it is unlikely to provoke a takeover raid, or the sacrifice is substantial enough that the risk of takeover is very real. Corporate social responsibility (CSR) seems to suggest that a firm should sacrifice profits only in the interest of some noneconomic objective in the first situation—that is, when the firm can confidently avoid takeover. But even when the risk of takeover is great, I do not believe the socially responsible firm can do nothing. If the firm decides that a profit sacrifice can come only at the risk of takeover, then it should use its influence to campaign for a change in the law that will oblige it to sacrifice profits but will prevent others from profiting by changing those decisions under the new order.

Are these differences sufficiently marginal that one is right to dismiss me as endorsing the critics of CSR? No. As Gates suggests, there are surely many situations in which companies can advance social objectives without a major sacrifice of profits. And it is wildly impractical to suggest that any and every time a firm faces a decision of this type it should demand a change in the law to force future managers to act in the social interest. If we were to legislate to oblige everyone to always act in the social interest, it would also spell the end of individual liberty. Of course, there will be some firms that abuse their privileges and seek to maximize profits whatever the social cost and however little the social benefit; if one believes in maximizing individual liberty, then one shrugs with regret and recognizes this as a cost. But one does not deny that there is sometimes a social cost or advocate that companies behave like brigands, as the critics of CSR seem to suggest.

The lobbying power of firms cuts in both directions. I do not doubt that some companies use their influence to campaign for changes that enhance profits and allow them to ride roughshod over other social objectives. But the companies that embrace CSR implicitly promise that they will not behave this way, and there is no reason why they shouldn't use their lobbying power to pursue socially beneficial changes in the law.

MY VERSION OF THE RIGHT KIND

Nancy Birdsall

It's always seemed to me that one of the best things that global firms operating in developing countries can do is a different sort of lobbying from what John Williamson suggests: lobbying for a level playing field, especially where the firms can resist "competitive" pressure and lobby for fair rules and effective enforcement.

(Whether this is creative capitalism by Gates's definition or anyone else's, I don't know. If the definition includes readiness to give up certain immediate profits for a bundle of less certain, higher future profits with possible high social benefits, then perhaps it ought to qualify.)

For example, a global firm operating in a pollution-producing sector might choose clean technology in a developing country where antipollution rules or enforcement are inadequate. It loses out to dirty local competitors in the short run, but uses its influence to push for better enforcement. Once those are in hand, its greater overall efficiency brings it greater market share and higher profits.

JUST TAX THE RICH

John Roemer

There are substantial moral objections to relying on a form of charity as the redress for excessive inequality. Many, myself included, believe that justice requires a far more equal distribution of income and material benefits than currently exists in the United States, let alone in the world. Repairing the present injustice should not be left to charity (or corporate philanthropy) but should instead be a state mandate.

The reasons for this should be familiar from arguments put forth years ago in Europe and the United States for replacing voluntarist schemes with a welfare state. It is unrealistic in the extreme to expect that wealthy capitalists will dispense as much wealth through corporate philanthropy as could be raised by a more redistributive system of taxation than we now have. And if, as I believe, the current distribution of wealth constitutes an injustice, what moral right do the corporate titans have to decide how that wealth should be used? If, in contrast, these funds were raised with taxes, then the public, through democratic institutions, would decide how to allocate it.

I will not attempt to justify my view that the highly unequal distribution of wealth and income in American capitalism constitutes an injustice (that has been argued elsewhere). Rather, I would like to argue that increasing taxes on the wealthy would not destroy incentives to work hard and therefore be inefficient.

Last spring, *The New York Times* published data assembled by economists Thomas Piketty and Emmanuel Saez showing that the richest 1 percent of American households in 2005 received 21.8 percent of the total income earned by Americans, a degree of concentration higher than in any year since 1928, when the richest 1 percent of households took in 23.9 percent of total income. In other words, these households earn (on average) 22 times as much as the average American household. But these very rich households are, on average, paupers compared to those who occupy the top one-tenth of 1 percent of the American income distribution: In 2004, that segment received 8.94 percent of total American income, or, on average, 89 times average household income. This degree of income concentration is unprecedented in advanced democracies. The top tenth of 1 percent in France received 1.62 percent of total French income in 2005, and in Britain, the most unequal advanced European democracy, the top tenth of 1 percent received 4.72 percent of total income.

In 1960, these superrich paid income taxes at over three times the average rate for all Americans; but in 2004, their average tax rate was only 1.3 times the average rate for all Americans. Thus, relatively speaking, the very rich have enjoyed a huge cut in income taxes over this forty-year period.

Why has pretax income become so concentrated at the very top, and why have tax rates diminished so drastically on those incomes, thus leaving a posttax distribution of income which is by far the most skewed among the advanced democracies? The concentration in pretax earnings at the top is in large part due to the huge salaries of CEOs, star athletes, and movie stars. There are those who argue that the mega-salaries of CEOs in the top corporations are the consequence of market imperfections or corruption, mutual back-scratching, and the like.

But this is not obviously the case. Competitive markets, if they work properly, assign incomes to workers (including CEOs) roughly equal to their marginal products. Suppose a firm like Wal-Mart, whose profits are on the order of $10 billion a year, is hiring a CEO. If the board of directors decides that the two top contenders are Alison and Bill and conjectures that manager Alison might bring in $10.4 billion while manager Bill a slightly smaller $10.2 billion, then it is estimating Alison's marginal product (what she brings to the firm over the next best contender) at $200 million. Alison should be able to bargain for a salary that takes a good portion of that extra $200 million, if she has attractive outside options. Even if she does not bargain very hard and takes only $50 million, Wal-Mart will have profited $150 million by hiring her over Bill.

So it may well be the case that the huge salaries of the CEOs of mega-corporations are not a sign of market imperfections or corruption, but are rather the outcome of the market working just the way the textbooks say it should. This does not mean either that Alison deserves a salary of $50 million or that she would refuse to supply her rare managerial talents for much less—say for $1 million. Alison's "reservation wage" will depend on what alternatives she has. In an unregulated market economy, she will have many alternatives that will keep her salary in the stratosphere.

Because there are many corporations that would bid for

Alison, her salary will almost certainly be large. There remains, however, a perfectly legal way to reduce Alison's taking, and that is to tax her income at a high rate. Indeed, if all countries that are homes to mega-corporations tax high incomes at a high rate, Alison's after-tax income will be considerably reduced, no matter where she works. At present, the main outlier in implementing this kind of tax policy is the United States— and, in fact, because we tax high incomes at a low rate, that puts pressure on other countries to do so as well, so that their mega-corporations can compete for the talents of Alison and her ilk. So the low tax rates that America imposes on the very rich may well induce a race to the bottom, where tax rates are reduced on the very rich everywhere. After all, if a country is to compete successfully in the world market, it needs innovative mega-corporations managed by the best talent available.

In the last thirty years, conservative think tanks, almost all in the United States, have propagated the view that such high after-tax incomes are necessary in order to elicit the talents of those like Alison. But this is a ridiculous claim. Suppose that, because of universally high tax rates in advanced democracies, Alison's take-home pay were only $5 million—although her market income might well remain at $50 million, due to competition among firms for her talents. Would Alison work less hard? Would she prefer to stay home by the pool and cultivate her tan?

Very unlikely. Alison is probably a workaholic who loves the power that is associated with managing a huge firm, loves producing products that millions of consumers want to purchase, and loves the accolades that she receives from her social set for a being a mover and shaker. Indeed, if everyone in her social set has a take-home income of "only" $5 million or so, her prestige will be just as great as it would be in the current low-tax world. For the fancy lifestyle that Alison pursues is not intended to reinvigorate her for the tough job she does: rather, it acts as a signal to the rest of the world of how important she is. That signal, and the psychological return Alison gets from the ensuing recognition, depend only upon her relative consumption, not her absolute consumption.

But the popular economic discourse is now dominated by the inefficiency of government and the importance of avoiding too much meddling with the market distribution of income, for fear of dampening the incentives for the highest fliers to put their scarce talents to use.

Yet the necessity of government intervention remains a critical task if America is to become a more just and solidaristic society. Markets, even if they work efficiently, will not produce a distribution of income that is just and in which those who earn the most would be perfectly willing to provide their productive services for far less income. High taxation of the rich would not only produce a more solidaristic society—by reducing the extreme differences in consumption that characterize contemporary American society—but would provide the government with income that could be used to vastly better the lives of the most disadvantaged through improved public education, improved access to health care, and the eradication of poverty directly, not to speak of the dedication of a larger fraction of our national income to foreign aid.

A CAPITALIST KNOWS WHO TO CALL

Abhijit Banerjee

I am frankly a little baffled by this conversation about the feasibility and/or moral justifiability of creative capitalism. Capitalism, after all, is a system that draws a lot of its strength from the fact that successful entrepreneurs end up with huge rents—not just normal profits on their equity but what some people would call obscene amounts of money. If those successful entrepreneurs want to "consume" their rents in the form of doing what they consider to be good for the world, who are we to tell them that they can't? Indeed, isn't a part of capitalist ideology that choice increases the value of money?

Why wouldn't we want to offer capitalists the choice of how they want to get their kicks? Shareholders might disapprove, I agree, but they can always take their money elsewhere or try to get the capitalist fired (board meetings exist for that purpose). My guess is that they mostly won't because the entrepreneurs who want to take on creative capitalism are precisely the entrepreneurs who have made tons of money for their shareholders.

The relevant question to me is whether it is a good idea: Would society be better off if the creative capitalists stuck to their day jobs, where they clearly are doing some good—creating jobs, serving customers, inventing new products—or would it be better off if they ventured into what is sometimes called the social sector?

I emphatically support the latter option. We want more creative capitalists. As I see it, one of the weaknesses of the capitalist model is also one of the things that make it so powerful: the huge incomes it offers those who make it to the top. The result is that young men and women of talent tend to find their way toward a job in the private sector, in part to make money, in part just to achieve a level of comfort comparable to that of their friends, in part to prove to themselves that they can do it. The flip side of this is that the rest of the economy, "the social sector," is always starved of talent and often ends up in the hands of those who are there because they could not cut it in the private sector. And, unfortunately, these are the parts of the economy that are meant to take care of the poor—making sure that no one falls below some acceptable standard of living and that every child has the chance to make it.

I don't mean to say that there are no talented people in government. But they are often frustrated, in part by the thin salaries, the process, and the poor quality of the people around them. As a result, there is a strong tendency, at least in the countries I know well, for talented people to leave the government or, what is even sadder, turn into the local cynics.

Which leaves the NGOs. I know a number of marvelous NGOs, but even the best of them are usually strapped for cash and frustrated by their inability to really take their best ideas to scale and change the way that the social sector functions. Now along comes Mr. Gates, and I hope many like him, backed by enough cash to give the ideas he likes (his own and those of others that he likes) a fair tryout and the political pull to make governments take them seriously. We could see a sea change in how social policy gets carried out. Add to that the fact that he knows how to run a large organization and how to get people excited about what they are doing and is free to set up the organizational culture and reward structure he wants, and we might be on the brink of a revolution in how social services get delivered.

There are, as I see it, two obvious objections to this optimistic vision. First, how do we know innovation is what the social sector needs today? Perhaps the fact that the government is organized the way it is acknowledges that innovation is not a priority and that it would be a waste to involve the best minds in the world in reinventing the delivery system.

This, I think, is pure nonsense. The remarkable thing about governments is how little they have changed organizationally over the last one hundred years despite the amazing progress we have seen in technology and the substantial, though less remarkable, progress made by the social sciences.

Take the example of curing TB. The basic technology for curing TB has been known for fifty years or more: Take lots of strong antibiotics regularly over several months, and don't stop taking them because you are feeling better. It has been twenty years since it was recognized that patient adherence to the drug regime was a major challenge and one important reason that so many people still died from TB. The World Health Organization (WHO) has been pushing the Directly Observed Therapy, Short-Course (DOTS) program as a solution to this problem for almost as long. The idea is that someone will be there to observe the patient taking the medicine every time he or she needs to take it.

It is clear that this is a rather cumbersome way around this problem; it works, but only if the observer is motivated, which is not guaranteed. Indeed, one of the more robust findings of the literature in social psychology (and more recently in economics) is that even with the best of intentions, people find it difficult to commit to do something slightly tedious, like going to the gym or resisting cookies, on a long-term basis. Observing someone every day is similar, and good intentions may not always be enough. And since in many instances the person doing the observing is a government employee, even the good intentions cannot be taken for granted. Another robust finding from the recent literature on service delivery is that government nurses in rural health centers (exactly the people who are supposed to be doing the observing in many countries) are absent a third of the time or more.

Mohammed Jameel, a genuine creative capitalist and an MIT alum, recently set up what he calls the Yunus challenge at MIT to honor his friend and fellow creative capitalist, Muhammad Yunus. Every year the Yunus challenge asks groups of MIT students to come up with designs that combine technology with insights from the social sciences to solve problems of social importance. We at the Jameel Poverty Action Lab get to suggest some of the problems students are asked to solve. Two years ago we challenged them to come up with an alternative to DOTS.

One group of students came back with what they called NEW DOTS. This involves adding a neutral reagent to the TB medicine that shows up in the urine of those who are taking their pills on schedule. They also came up with strips that react to the reagent in the urine by revealing a code. By calling in the right code to the right number at the right time, people earn credit, which can be redeemed later.

The idea, obviously, is to give people a small reward for taking the pill on schedule, and there is a growing body of research that suggests small rewards can be quite powerful as a way to overcome people's tendency to procrastinate.

The point here is not to extol the brilliance of MIT students (though they are brilliant). It is to ask why all this was not old hat, why a hundred such models were not coming out of government research cells all over the world every year, given the known difficulties with the DOTS approach. The answer, obviously, is that this is not how governments think, which is why I firmly believe the social sector could do with an infusion of creative talent from outside.

The creative capitalist has a real advantage; he knows how to put pressure on governments and how to market his ideas to the man in the street. He has credibility, he does not need anyone else's money, and he knows who to call. I think something good is about to happen.

DOES FOREIGN AID CREATE WEAK STATES?

Michael Kremer

One issue that has come up in this discussion is the impact of aid on developing countries. Richard Posner's skepticism about creative capitalism seems to stem in part from a larger skepticism about aid. But is that skepticism warranted?

Standard economic theory would suggest that providing developing countries with a steady transfer of 5 percent of our GDP each year would allow consumption in those countries to be approximately 5 percent higher than it would have been otherwise. That won't turn your average developing country into Korea, but for someone earning under a dollar a day, a 5 percent increase in consumption can make the difference between education and ignorance or malnourishment and health. Indeed, the developing world, including most of Africa, has seen tremendous improvements in literacy and reductions in infant mortality in recent decades, a fact that often gets lost in discussions about aid.

Inventive minds can come up with exotic stories about why aid might have a much bigger or much smaller effect than the standard theory suggests. Jeff Sachs promotes a poverty trap theory: Receiving a little bit of aid allows countries to start domestic investments moving into a virtuous cycle of self-sustaining growth. Richard Posner and others can tell complicated stories about why aid leads to worse domestic institutions and reduces growth. Both of these theories are possible—and there may be specific cases in which they have been borne out—but there is no good evidence of either theory being generally applicable.

In this discussion, no one has taken Sachs's position that aid could have a growth-enhancing effect, so I won't address that issue, but Richard Posner has suggested that aid leads to worse government, and I believe that suggestion is wrong. Once we set aside the question of what impact aid has when it is given for geopolitical reasons (e.g., aid to Egypt or Pakistan), there seems to be, if anything, good reason to believe that development aid actually improves the quality of government.

First, apart from places of strategic importance, donors typically avoid giving aid to the worst governments. Zimbabwe doesn't get a lot.

Second, there are both left- and right-wing critiques of aid, and it is hard to reconcile their arguments about why aid is harmful. The standard left-wing critique of the World Bank and the International Monetary Fund (IMF) is that these organizations make aid conditional on lowering tariffs, privatizing state-run industries, adopting conservative monetary policy, and so on. And it's true: A lot of foreign aid has been made contingent on these domestic policy changes. Over the past few decades there have been dramatic reductions in average tariff levels, a huge reduction in the number of countries that restrict access to foreign exchange for imports (an important generator of corruption and political patronage), and a virtual elimination of hyperinflation. Zimbabwe is the exception that proves the rule.

It seems likely that aid has played a role in some of these trends. But, at a minimum, there seems to be a strange disconnect between this leftist story about aid and the critics in this discussion, who condemn aid because it supposedly causes countries to move away from free-market policies and toward bloated governments that meddle too often with their economies. And, at a maximum, it seems possible that the much-maligned "Washington consensus" in fact played a very useful role. If the IMF can take even a small fraction of the credit for India's early-'90s reforms, it's probably earned its keep for a while.

More recently, donors have promoted democracy along with free markets, which probably has something to do with the small wave of democracy that has swept over Africa.

Finally, aid institutions themselves create important career incentives for people in developing countries. The presence of international aid organizations means that a local civil servant who is trying to be honest has some alternative employment besides his national government. As Ed Glaeser points out, the visible existence of alternative power structures is likely to be salutary for a developing nation's political culture and economic development. And the World Bank has helped produce a series of finance ministers, presidents, and prime ministers who have implemented important reforms in countries from Liberia to Turkey.

But overall, it's hard to know what the political effect of aid is. It has had some spectacular successes, like the green revolution and the eradication of smallpox, and it has certainly had its share of failures as well. It seems best to judge aid efforts on a case-by-case basis, rather than with a general theory—be it that aid is critical to escaping poverty or that it sustains dictators.

And even if you think aid from governments can undermine political institutions, creative capitalism is likely to have fewer potential negative effects. If a firm invents a new drug or vaccine to fight tropical disease, or launches a mobile-phone-based banking service, it will directly help millions of people. It seems a bit churlish to criticize the firm based on a theoretical possibility that doing so may lead to dictatorship.

YES, BUT WEAK STATES CAN BE COAXED CREATIVELY

Eric Werker

Creative capitalism has the most work to do in weak states, where poor institutions impede the political process, misdirect the private sector, and produce terrible education and health outcomes. Indeed, as Professor Glaeser argues, one of the best things creative capitalists can do in the face of missing government is to step in and pick up the slack. But weak states today have lots of qualities that could keep creative capitalism from saving the day—in the worst case, creative capitalism could just add to the problem.

In the weakest states, the status quo is certainly grim. According to the Human Development Report, the life expectancy in Sierra Leone is less than 42 years. The female literacy rate in Chad is less than 13 percent. The richest 10 percent in the Central African Republic "earn" nearly 70 times more income than the poorest 10 percent. These places seem like the ideal ground for creative capitalism to turn things around. But in weak states, government has been broken by decades of war, coups, colonial extraction, and corruption. Business has captured the state, or vice versa. Can we expect creative capitalism to work when government institutions are so bad?

The usual ways to unleash the energy of capitalism run into problems in weak states. One can't rely on government regulations to drive private sector activity toward social ends when government regulators are totally corrupt. Similarly, one can't hope that "recognition" profits will change business practices to the point where Gap or Intel will open up manufacturing facilities in places like Somalia or Timor-Leste. And the few firms already operating there are not going to act more socially responsible to enhance their reputations in the developed world.

So what about creative nonprofits or foundations? When these organizations provide goods and services in weak states, without a doubt they make life a little bit better to the people they serve. But like applying a Band-Aid to a broken arm, this type of entrepreneurial altruism can miss the point: The main problem is that the state is not providing those goods and services. When a foundation funds the private provision of anti-retroviral medicine, the corrupt leaders of a weak state do not think: "What a great idea!" Instead, they gain a free move in the slow war of attrition they wage against their people.

Should we ask private firms operating in weak states to behave in a more socially responsible fashion? As Professor Easterly points out, that can't exist on a big enough scale to make a dent in global poverty. But in a small, weak state with few large businesses, we can imagine pressuring, or funding, a small majority of firms to uphold a higher standard of social responsibility.

HOW THE AID INDUSTRY GOT CREATIVE

Nancy Birdsall

This discussion of creative capitalism has featured a variety of pieces on the effects of foreign aid—with views ranging from support to skepticism to outright hostility. But no one has pointed out that the aid "industry" writ large (including not just the official practitioners but the academics and think tankers who scrutinize it) has also gotten creative lately—creative about new ways to transfer aid money that exploit market mechanisms and harness the power of capitalism.

The most notable example is the advance market commitment, discussed earlier by Michael Kremer. But there are others. For at least three decades, for example, USAID has supported "social marketing" of contraceptives. In very poor areas, contraceptives are priced (with some subsidy) and distributed through normal wholesale and retail networks—in other words, through the robust distribution channels that the market generates organically.

Others have suggested using fiscal policy tools to promote individual involvement in foreign aid. Eric Werker, for instance, has proposed using domestic tax deductions to generate incentives for new investments in the world's poorest countries. That would be creative use of the government's tax power to address the information problems and market failures that limit U.S. investors' interest in small, poor economies, like Mali and Ghana, where there is a potential for high-return investment.

And there is a new wave of interest in "results-based" and "output-based" aid, both of which subsidize development projects using a mechanism similar to the advance market commitment for vaccines: The funding is all performance-based. These policies are meant to increase the efficiency and effectiveness of aid money.

And why shouldn't donors invite recipient countries to go the private capital markets and securitize promised future aid flows? The market would reveal useful—and possibly embarrassing—information about the credibility of aid promises.

EVEN GOVERNMENT CAN BE CREATIVE

Michael Kremer

Much of this discussion has focused on what firms can and can't do to address problems of poverty in the developing world. This is all to the good. However, governments can also open opportunities for the private sector to help provide health and education in the developing world. There are lots of good examples.

Take health. Incentives for public sector teachers and health workers in developing countries are often extraordinarily weak. A survey of schools and health clinics in Bangladesh, Ecuador, India, Indonesia, Peru, and Uganda found that teachers were absent from their schools 19 percent of the time and health workers were absent from the clinics 35 percent of the time. And even when teachers and health workers were in their schools and clinics, they weren't necessarily working. Public school teachers in India are in class and teaching only half the time.

These public sector teachers are paid well above the market rate, earning four times as much as teachers in many rural private schools. The issue is not low wages but weak incentives.

Only one out of three thousand headmasters in a recent survey reported knowing of a teacher who had been fired for absence, despite an epidemic of absenteeism.

I have been involved in evaluating two programs in which governments sought to encourage private sector participation in education and health. In these programs the government still funded the provisions and set the rules of the game—they just used the private sector as a delivery mechanism. Colombia's Plan de Ampliación de Cobertura de la Educación Secundaria (PACES) program provided scholarships to allow children from poor neighborhoods who had attended public primary schools to attend private secondary schools. The amount of the scholarship was comparable (actually less) than it would have cost to provide public secondary education.

More people applied for scholarships than could be supported with the available funds, so lotteries were used to allocate voucher slots. Josh Angrist, Eric Bettinger, Erik Bloom, Elizabeth King, and I compared education outcomes for lottery losers and winners to isolate the impact of the program from other factors like family background. We found that, three years after the original application process, the lottery winners scored higher on tests and progressed through higher grades than the losers did.

Eric, Josh, and I also obtained records on the high school graduation/college entrance exam in Colombia. About 30 percent of lottery losers managed to complete high school and take this exam, but lottery winners were 5 to 7 percentage points more likely to do so. Our best estimates suggest that the program led to substantial improvements in test scores as well.

In health care, a voucher program would likely be less successful, due to the severe problems that afflict private fee-for-service health care provisions. The private fee-for-service sector is huge in many developing countries, since many people do not want to go to public clinics.

And while incentives for providers in the private sector are strong, they are often poorly aligned with the needs of patients, let alone public health needs, because of information asymmetries between customers and providers. Many providers have no formal medical training whatsoever. These are not traditional healers, just people who have set themselves up in the business of dispensing drugs without medical qualifications. Such providers have incentives to make the patient feel better in the short run—by providing glucose drips or steroid shots—but not necessarily to do what's best for the patient's long-term health, let alone for public health. There is inadequate incentive for private fee-for-service providers to supply services that have public health benefits for society as a whole, such as vaccination.

In 1999, Cambodia tried a new approach: It contracted out management of government health services in five districts. Contractors took over management of government health centers, and their performance was measured against eight service-delivery indicators, related primarily to maternal and child health. Once they took over management, contractors typically strengthened incentives for staff, offering extra pay for good performance and restricting or prohibiting staff from moonlighting in private practice on the side.

The districts chosen for contracting were selected randomly from a larger set, making it possible to rigorously evaluate the project by comparing treatment and outcomes between districts. The project created large improvements in the eight targeted health outcomes and had generally positive effects for other outcomes, suggesting that contractors were not gaming the system by shifting resources into measured outcomes. For example, in contracted districts, delivery of vitamin A to children under age five increased by 21 percentage points and delivery of antenatal or postbirth care to pregnant women by 33 percentage points.

During surprise visits, it was 61 percent more likely that all scheduled staff were present in contracted health centers than in uncontracted health centers, and contracted health centers were better stocked with supplies and equipment. In response to the improved service, district residents reduced visits to unqualified drug sellers and traditional healers and increased visits to qualified staff in public facilities. This change in care-seeking behavior lowered out-of-pocket private health spending, offsetting the increase in public spending associated with the project.

Such contracting programs offer the opportunity to strengthen incentives for health care workers while reducing potentially harmful incentives associated with private fee-for-service approaches. Contracting at the district level allows for competition between providers in different districts.

Similar contracting approaches have been carried out on a large scale (covering 50,000 to 30 million individuals) in nine countries. By creating programs along the lines of Colombia's school choice program or Cambodia's health care contracting program, governments can spur entrepreneurs to undertake the type of creative capitalism Bill Gates called for in Davos.

DON'T CHANGE CAPITALISM, EXPAND IT

Kyle Chauvin

The call for something called creative capitalism reflects a recognition that market incentives hold the potential to solve problems that baffle even the most concerted efforts of philanthropy and state action. But what comes out of that recognition seems to me a bit odd: a call for capitalism, as practiced in advanced economies that already practice it best, to be changed or fixed. Before we devote a lot of energy to reforming capitalism at home, where it already works pretty well, maybe we should devote more effort to extending capitalism's reach in places where it hasn't yet fully flowered.

If this smacks pretty sourly of Western intellectual arrogance, outdated Cold War tactics, and this country's more recent attempts at nation building, let me be clear: That's not what I mean. As purely a tool of problem solving and an answer to the challenge of wealth creation, capitalism has been shown to be enormously effective. But capitalism can't function without certain institutions, and those institutions need to be built. The most creative thing businesses in advanced economies can do is to help spread capitalism—

traditional, textbook, supply-and-demand capitalism—in the developing world.

The defining feature of capitalism is that it tackles grand-scale problems with decentralized, Schumpeterian trial and error—it's a method of allocating resources that's remarkably efficient, flexible, and even creative. We know now that capitalism is not, as used to be alleged, a cultural phenomenon of the West. It has worked in such varied environments as South Korea, Hong Kong, Israel, and Peru. And capitalism need not be justified in ideological terms, especially as its opposite, centralized economic decision making, is now a proven disaster. Rather, what constrains the ability of individuals to participate in markets in much of the underdeveloped world today is a host of individual factors—namely, disease, starvation, lack of education, violence, larceny, state persecution, international barriers to trade, absence of credit, restrictive monopolies, and insufficiently defined property rights (and I am probably forgetting a few).

In the debate over creative capitalism, we ought to be asking: What is the optimal role for business to play in reducing these impediments? In the arsenal of potential strategies, where does the private sector hold a philanthropic comparative advantage? One very obvious answer was proposed by Professor Landsburg: Business can sever itself from the protectionist lobby. Nothing else could be done with so little time and effort. Another easy answer is almost counterintuitive: Businesses can continue to scan the globe for the cheapest sources of labor, using their profit-motivated research to effectively bring wages to those who need them the most (and who are precisely those who will accept the least).

Other solutions require, well, a bit of creativity.

Microlending is the most familiar example. Providing the smallest-scale investments to ordinary individuals, this nascent industry is helping to foster the trial and error (or "searching" for solutions, in the terminology of Professor Easterly) that lies at the heart of capitalism. As recent reports have shown, microlending is not necessarily a philanthropic activity and is being propelled by the classic motive of profit.

However, there are ways that multinational corporations can help bring capitalism to underdeveloped countries other than opening new lines of business. One example that is still in the wishful thinking stage is property rights. Large multinational corporations may be better equipped to gather the information necessary to establish a regime of property rights than either government or private individuals. The correlation between economic prosperity and property rights is pretty much undisputed, but the direction of the causal arrow is up for debate. Hernando de Soto and the Peruvian Institute for Liberty and Democracy have argued strongly that formal property rights cause economic growth. If you buy this, then one way to deploy "creative capitalism" is to solve the problem of inadequate property rights.

The ability of individuals and firms to participate in a market is constrained by how much is known about who else is participating, who owns what, where it is, and how it can be used. Without this information, production, trade, and innovation are still possible but hampered, and markets are whittled down to single communities (or worse: single families). Individuals with physical property don't have the legal documentation (legal title, deeds, et cetera) that would allow them to borrow against the property. A system of credit is essential for the growth of more sophisticated financial markets. Trade with the developed world is impeded by an inability to "link up" with the already functioning information systems of Western firms. Domestically, the isolating effect of the lack of information hinders the division of labor, which is absolutely vital for efficiency. Finally, ignorance (or, as much, common distrust) by market insiders prevents outsiders from accurately evaluating the economy.

A solution to this problem would necessarily involve both the collection of information and measures to guarantee its validity (i.e., legal protection). The private sector (especially foreign businesses) might well be better than national governments at the first task. The ability to gather, organize, and process large amounts of information in an efficient manner is one natural by-product of a successful multinational, and competitive, entity. What's needed, as I understand it, is a census of property. Employers could, without much additional cost, help to ensure that employees and their relatives are included in this census, and if need be, employers could physically carry out parts of the process.

Would this task be done more efficiently if it were under the control of government? Almost certainly, the answer to this is no: The alternative to businesses, already equipped with databases of their workers and facing a low marginal cost of fleshing them out, is governmental bureaucracy, of whose record the best thing to be said is nothing at all. Would governments perhaps perform the task more fairly? There is clearly the possibility of twisted incentives for multinationals to underrate some and overrate others in an effort to aid their friends. But I imagine the same temptation exists, and is likely even stronger, for underpaid bureaucrats with strong local ties.

Why would companies want to go through with this? Maybe

a creative capitalist would take on this project for all of the nonfinancial reasons discussed by others in this blog. But generous impulses or a hunger for recognition may not even be necessary. The company's long-term profit might well be increased (at least in expectation) through the avoidance of additional governmental regulation and negative public sentiment.

To return to a broader perspective, the challenge before us is not to amend a broken system—capitalism, where it works, works as well as it ever has—but rather to identify which elements of this system give rise to its seemingly magical rate of progress and to find ways of propagating them further. If that means corporate social responsibility, then let's have corporate social responsibility. But let's keep in mind that much of the world still struggles to enjoy the basic elements of capitalism. The most creative thing we could do is to address this problem and leave experiments with the more baroque variations on capitalism for later.

THE LESSON OF HISTORY
Gregory Clark

Previously, I joined Gary Becker, Richard Posner, and others in rejecting Bill Gates's proposal for "creative capitalism." But on reflection I am also attracted to elements of the position that Michael Kremer has advanced—that nonpecuniary motives can be very powerful and could be productively harnessed by modern profit-driven corporations. Indeed, any attempt to tell the history of the Industrial Revolution and the rise of the modern world in purely Chicago school terms—as the unleashing of the profit motive by free competition—fails. The innovative firms at the heart of the modern Industrial Revolution depended as much on idealism, pride, and the search for fame as they did on the desire to make money.

The source of economists' unease about creative capitalism is an intuition that it is desirable to separate decisions about production from those on consumption. Andrew Carnegie was a model of this separation: a shark as a businessman, successfully breaking the union in the bloody Homestead Strike, but a benevolent uncle as a philanthropist.

Modern capitalism does seem to find that the profit motive

works marvelously well in supplying goods. Even goods that most find repugnant get produced in abundance: cigarettes for the nicotine addicted, Hummers for the gasoline addicted, and powerful guns for Rambo fans.

But capitalism was not always so. The first hundred years of the Industrial Revolution produced extraordinarily little in the way of profits for the innovators who created the modern world. Protection of intellectual property rights was weak. Even most of the innovators whose names we know—James Hargreaves, Samuel Crompton, Edmund Cartwright—gained little. And these were the success stories.

Fortunately, while profit partly drove innovation, as important was the romance of technology, patriotism, and the desire for fame. In a famous example, the miner's safety lamp, which greatly expanded the coal seams in which miners could work, was developed by Humphry Davy as a humanitarian venture. He refused to take any profit from the innovation. However, he did squabble furiously and selfishly with George Stephenson as to who deserved the glory for the innovation.

The message of history is this: Companies that can align their activities with solving humanity's problems should find that they can hire people of greater talent, at lower prices, than companies that seem to pander only to people's baser desires. A Detroit auto industry that, for example, focused on developing vehicles with less CO_2 emissions and greater safety should be able to recruit a lot more talent more cheaply than an industry currently identified with peddling polluting monster toys to the testosterone addled.

Of course, as is always the case with advice about economics, the question is, Why don't firms already know this? Why would they need Bill Gates to remind them of what they should already know?

The answer is that in modern markets, which often have few producers and entry barriers, firms can lose sight of fundamental truths. Those with confidence in the ability of the market to always figure out the most profitable strategy have to ignore the astonishing changes of strategy pursued by U.S. firms over the years, many of which have been fueled by no more than management fads: merger waves followed by divestiture waves; modestly compensated chief executives followed by emirs who plunder the corporate treasury. To a surprising extent, U.S. capitalism is following a course charted by competing gurus of the firm. Bill Gates's call has as much possibility of being a socially productive insight as the latest management infatuation to emerge from Harvard Business School.

So two cheers for creative capitalism. Would it work? Who knows? But since corporate America seems to need the direction of some new dogma, why not experiment with one that honors the better impulses of the citizenry?

GATES: THE RIGHT PLACE AT THE RIGHT TIME

Nancy Koehn

Gates has earned our ear (and for many of us, our respect) largely because he succeeded so convincingly playing the game of market capitalism that first emerged in the late nineteenth century and grew to great influence during the twentieth century. This game or system has been dominated in many industries by large, multinational corporations that compete intensively—usually with a small number of rivals—for market power. (Indeed, at the Harvard Business School, where I have taught business history to thousands of MBAs, students often compare the early growth of Standard Oil to that of Microsoft one hundred years later. They also compare John D. Rockefeller to Gates, arguing that both entrepreneurs saw the outlines of competition in their respective industries before other players and could thus act quickly to create and control what become the standards of rivalry in each young market). The economic spoils of this system have been valued and distributed in different ways—through employment patterns, market share, business investment, and most prominently, stock market performance.

Given Gates's achievements, it is interesting that he is throwing down a gauntlet to have global capitalism direct itself toward social contribution as well as financial gain. It is also important. Viewed through the lens of history, there are five powerful forces working on the system of global capitalism in this moment, propelling it along the broad path that Gates sketched out at Davos.

The first is the issue of resources. Who has what to deal with the pressing challenges today? If we think solely about resources—people, innovation, traction, money, and execution—business is the most powerful force for change on the global stage right now. No other set of institutions—not religious organizations, not the nation-state, not individual NGOs—has the resources or the breadth and on-the-ground depth of business to deal with what is front of us today. Yes, all these other players matter, in some cases a great deal. But not as much as business—in the form of both large, global corporations and small-scale entrepreneurial enterprises. This is not philosophy or politics, but the ineluctable reality of our moment.

A second force affecting the speed and direction of global capitalism comes from the demand side. There are millions—soon to be billions—of consumers, voters, and other actors, most obviously "millennials," who want something new and different from business, who conceive of business and the "flywheel" of global capitalism in ways distinctive from their counterparts of the past (and indeed in ways different from many boomers today). These actors will exert great power in the next two decades.

At the same time, the corporate form is changing very fast. New networks of companies and organizations are emerging; new ways of competing and collaborating are becoming more important. Old boundaries are withering. The traditional widget-making company maximizing its own profit in a nationally defined space is evolving into something more complex and much more integrated into a broad, often global, web of relationships.

A fourth catalyst is transparency. Leaders and organizations of all kinds are increasingly operating in glass houses. The explosion in transparency wrought by a global media, great leaps in connectivity, a generation of global citizens who demand novel commitments from business are creating new standards of conduct for even those actors least willing to change.

Finally, though less obviously, there is a palpable thirst among people around the world for leadership that is not for sale, for individuals and organizations that are not solely defined by the transactional rhythms and white-hot speed of the marketplace. (My graduating MBA students talk of this concern frequently as they discuss job choices and sketch out their own career plans.) We can see this in the enduring popularity of entrepreneurial leaders such as Warren Buffett and Oprah Winfrey, individuals who have thrived in their respective industries partly because they consistently pursued something more then the next market-dictated score.

All of these forces are gaining strength now and helping lay the pavement along which global capitalism will travel. This is evident in the success of large companies such as Costco, Jordan's Furniture, Southwest Airlines, Google, and even Starbucks, businesses that meet the needs of a broader set of stakeholders than shareholders. (A recent study of thirty such firms, by Rajendra Sisodia, David Wolfe, and Jag Sheth and published by the Wharton School, demonstrated that the public companies in this group returned 1,026 percent for investors over the 10 years ending June 20, 2006, while the S&P 500 returned 122 percent.)

The importance of these five forces is also evident in the young enterprises that are now beginning to exert themselves. Entrepreneurs and their creations have always been the sinews of capitalism. So we can look to organizations like RED, founded by Bono and Bobby Shriver, or Kiva—the online microlender created by two Stanford grads, Matt and Jessica Jackley Flannery—as important examples of where global capitalism is going. RED integrates the power of big business, new customer priorities, and the interconnected agents of social change, in the form of the Global Fund to Fight AIDS, Tuberculosis and Malaria. The animating mission of RED is to harness two of the most potent forces operating today, business and consumer spending, in the service of eradicating deadly diseases in Africa. Kiva connects small lenders—many of whom lend $50 or less—with promising entrepreneurs, mostly in developing countries. Three years after its founding, Kiva has helped fund more than 18,000 entrepreneurs in places like Samoa and Ecuador. This is creative; this is capitalism; and this is the future, right here on our doorstep.

WHAT MAKES CAPITALISM WORK?

Jagdish Bhagwati

Capitalism flourishes, even in the teeth of inevitable inequality, when one of five conditions exists:

First, it flourishes if the poor do not envy or resent the rich because they believe in the myth that they too can get rich. So if Bob Rubin and George Soros double their wealth and income on Park Avenue in New York City and the poor in Harlem notice it, they will think: ah, the size of the Lotto has gone up!

Second, it flourishes even if the poor do not buy into the upward mobility myth, if the rich do not flaunt their wealth by practicing an ostentatious style of living. This was true of Simon Schama's Dutch burghers in his book *The Embarrassment of Riches,* and it has been true of the Jains in my home state of Gujarat, where billionaires often cannot be distinguished from the lower classes because they dress simply and drive small cars. You cannot resent what you do not see!

Third, it flourishes if the poor feel that the riches are deserved or legitimate. Bill Gates has done something remarkable, which most everyone admires. By contrast, George Soros made money from speculation, which most people hold in low esteem.

True, Bill Gates arouses animosities in Europe because of the antitrust case; but that is still a boutique phenomenon compared to the huge adulation almost everywhere. By contrast, Soros is admired in that strange land of former East European countries to which he directed many of his funds; he is far from being admired elsewhere. On campuses in the U.S., we are all under instructions not to criticize him for the rubbish that he peddles, for fear that we may lose a contribution; but Gates would draw admiring crowds.

Fourth, capitalism flourishes if wealth is not used for intrusion into politics. The contrast between Gates and Soros is dramatic in this regard.

Fifth, related to point two, it flourishes if the rich spend their money not on themselves but on social projects. Typically, for instance, the rich in Gujarat spent money on people's education, on health, and (believe it or not) even on agricultural extension and dry farming experiments. Their motto was: Create wealth, but spend it on the needy others, not on oneself.

Apropos this, what CSR (corporate social responsibility) does is to extend the traditional practice of the Burghers-Jains-Calvinists—where families that made the money spent it directly on social projects—to the corporations. CSR is the modern counterpart of the wonderful family-owned businesses.

And as this ethos grows, it may even be financially rewarding to pursue CSR: Good firms manage today to attract better staff (who want their firms to be socially responsible) and may even get a little premium in the marketplace from consumers (though the evidence for this is limited to people paying more for organic foods, for instance).

For me, these observations define what would make for a robust capitalism. And a robust capitalism would help us to reap all the dynamic, wealth-generating energies of capitalism that Marx wrote about and only the faux Marxists today deny or deplore.

IN DEFENSE OF A GOOD REPUTATION, PART TWO

Nancy Birdsall

Note that the Janus face of recognition is shame. When corporations go global, their leadership is less vulnerable to the shame that can be generated by neighbors and friends. It may be that at the local level the risk of shame carries greater weight than the benefits of recognition, because the risks are more specific and personal. The fear of shame that is local surely helps explain personal contributions by "small-town" corporate leaders to local culture or corporate sponsorship of the local Little League team.

I interpret Bill Gates's plea for more creative capitalism as an implicit acknowledgment that local shame is a less powerful force for social progress in a globalized market. The incentives for a multinational corporation—a corporation whose workers, shareholders, and customers are scattered around the world— to forgo expected profits in the interest of social gains are limited. That's all the more the case in settings where a company is unlikely to get what it deserves because of a sour history or where shame—local or global—does not affect their bottom line. (Think of Shell producing oil in Nigeria, compared to Nike and Nestlé producing consumer goods; the latter did get shamed at the global level and now seek recognition.)

That in turn suggests that creative capitalism thrives best where there are disinterested global monitors, ready to inflict shame as well as bestow recognition. The United Nations Global Compact is a program that corporations can sign up for, under which they promise to behave responsibly and to advance various social causes. The point is to threaten shame as well as bestow recognition. But there is not any monitoring or scrutiny of signatories' behavior by credible third parties (and the United Nations itself lacks sufficient credibility). As a result, the value is limited—so limited that one wonders why corporations take the trouble to sign up in the first place.

YOU WANT CREATIVE CAPITALISM? TRY THIS

Lawrence Summers

Here is a really good creative capitalism idea. All Americans benefit from increases in home ownership because of the values like hard work, community, and respect for property that ownership instills. Families want desperately to own their own homes and accumulate equity. Yet it is very hard for conventional banks that borrow money over the short term to lend over the kind of thirty-year horizon that best helps families buy houses.

How can the objective of ownership be best supported, and how can the most adequate financing be assured? Voilà, creative capitalism! How about chartering private companies as government-sponsored enterprises with the mission of promoting home ownership affordability? Give them boards with some private representatives and some public representatives. Make it clear that government stands behind their capital market innovations so they can borrow more cheaply and pass the savings on. Exempt them from the state and local taxes that others pay. Give them specific objectives on affordability that they must meet. Rely on a special government regulator to ensure that they balance their social responsibility with their drive to profit. Harness the profit motive to meet a social objective.

This is roughly the rationale behind Fannie Mae and Freddie Mac. I would submit that it is about as good or as bad as most creative capitalism ideas involving joint profit making and social objectives. But one hopes that we are now witnessing the end of this particular experiment in creative capitalism: The government is moving to pick up the pieces of the mess the government-sponsored enterprises have made, and their shareholders are losing most of their money.

What went wrong? The illusion that the companies were doing virtuous work made it impossible to build a political case for serious regulation. When there were social failures, the companies always blamed their need to perform for the shareholders. When there were business failures, it was always the result of their social obligations. Government budget discipline was not appropriate because it was always emphasized that they were "private companies." But market discipline was nearly nonexistent, given the general perception, now validated, that their debt was government-backed. Little wonder, with gains privatized and losses socialized, that the enterprises have gambled their way into financial catastrophe.

I wonder how general the lesson here might be. My fear is fairly general. Inherent in the multiple objectives urged for creative capitalists is a loss of accountability with respect to performance. The sense that the mission is virtuous is always a great club for beating down skeptics. When institutions have special responsibilities, it is necessary that they be supported in competition to the detriment of market efficiency.

It is hard in this world to do well. It is hard to do good. When I hear a claim that an institution is going to do both, I reach for my wallet. You should too.

A Reply to Summers:
YES, IT'S A FAIR WARNING
Vernon Smith

Larry Summers speaks well for many of us who have long thought of Fannie Mae and Freddie Mac as ticking time bombs. And he is right to see these as cautionary examples of creative capitalism. So before we go embrace Gates's idea, we should realize that we've just witnessed one of these creative capitalism time bombs go off. There is nothing intrinsically wrong with lending long (even thirty years for a house), borrowing short, and refinancing the short-term borrowing again and again to cover the thirty-year loan. It's just that success in such an endeavor requires more stability in the economic environment than it is likely can be delivered. In particular, such contracting arrangements and the institutions designed to carry them out have not fared well historically.

They do not weather deflationary or inflationary shocks:

- The savings and loan crisis of the 1980s and 1990s was an example of lending strains that ruptured into an S&L earthquake, created fundamentally by inflation.

• The recession and deflation of the 1930s precipitated a wave of foreclosures on homes, businesses, and farms. And many of the banks that foreclosed did not remain solvent because the foreclosed property was worth less in the market than the outstanding loans. Both parties to these contracts took hits.

There is a standard rule that long ago emerged in the creative world of capitalism to provide a reasonable means of insuring against such events: It's called equity. When a bank or mortgage institution lends long, it lends only a fraction of the market value of the asset and requires that the asset owner provide the remaining equity. As a result, it has a cushion to guard against default by the long borrower, whose foreclosed asset has a market value less than the long loan.

But here's the rub: The longer the loan and the greater the uncertainty of a stable economic environment, the greater the required upfront equity, or down payment. Taken to the limit, these factors can result in no one giving you a loan. No one is to blame, and intervention by a government agency to reduce the risk to the mortgage lender does nothing to reduce the reality of the risk to society.

Home buyers, who are also voters, don't like to accept that reality. Neither do the politicians who want to get elected and convince themselves, just as the potential home owners convince themselves, that you can get something for nothing—that you can obtain low-down-payment loans on home purchases and avoid the inherent risks.

These risks hold for all assets—almost all new inventions, products, and businesses are not loan-worthy—but homes represent a universally popular asset. Hence the emergence of the uneconomical but politically popular (and now discredited) government-sponsored enterprises (GSEs): Fannie Mae and Freddie Mac.

In this episode Fannie May and Freddie Mac assisted in their own demise by providing fuel for the mother of all housing bubbles. Our housing consumption binge is now over and there is more than enough blame and souring loans to spread around.

This bubble had significant new features. Topping my list: In 1997, President Clinton signed into law the Tax Relief Act (sponsored by Republicans in both houses) with overwhelming bipartisan support. This law allowed all of us to take a tax-free capital gain of up to a half-million dollars on homes sold.

Enter the financial market innovators, who pushed mortgage securitization as a mechanism for generating more liquid national markets for mortgages and helped us all become tax-free half-millionaires by selling our homes. Their so-called agency problem (as well as that of Fannie Mae and Freddie Mac) is just economic jargon for bad incentives to provide investors with a little packaged truth about real economic risk—risk that was historically recognized in the sizable down payment requirements.

But in the wave of a tax-free, get-rich-quick bubble, what is the truth? If builders, buyers, realtors, lenders, and mortgage packagers all think their asset prices will be higher tomorrow, then the downside risk is beyond perception and we have a widespread agency problem with ourselves. The creativity of traditional due diligence is swept aside.

Politically, correcting this will be even harder than getting rid of the ethanol subsidy for corn. But it's time to phase out Fannie Mae and Freddie Mac—let them go the way of the S&L.

Also, if you are going to insist that the consumer-durable

good called "housing" enjoy tax-free capital gains status, then please extend this provision to apply to all assets. If you sweeten only one asset, then you can expect capital to flood into that asset exactly as we have witnessed! Or, better yet, ignore the distinction between capital gains and income and allow all saving/investment to be deducted from income for tax purposes.

MAXIMIZING WHOSE PROFIT?

Justin Fox

There's already been ample discussion here of Milton Friedman's famous argument in "The Social Responsibility of Business Is to Increase Its Profits." But I haven't seen any explicit mention of the possibly more influential academic paper inspired by Friedman's essay: Michael Jensen and William Meckling's 1976 "Theory of the Firm: Managerial Behavior, Agency Costs and Ownership Structure."

I'm guessing that's because Jensen-Meckling is mostly a business school phenomenon, and there don't seem to be a lot of business school types involved in this effort. I'm not a business school type, but I am finishing a book in which Jensen plays a major role. So here's a quick history: Michael Jensen was a young finance professor at the University of Rochester's business school; William Meckling was the dean. Jensen had recently earned a doctorate at Chicago's business school, where he'd been a core member of the group of students and faculty who formulated and amassed evidence to support the efficient market hypothesis, the theory that stock prices "fully reflect available information." (Or, as one of Jensen's Rochester colleagues liked to put it: "The price is right.") Meckling was a former Chicago economics graduate student of Friedman (he never got around to getting his PhD but seemed to do just fine without it).

Jensen and Meckling read Friedman's piece in *The New York Times Magazine* in 1970, thought it was swell, and decided to translate it into the mathematical language of economics. In doing so, they quickly realized that while Friedman had written of corporate executives as "agents" who were supposed to look out for the interests of their owners, those agents faced all sorts of economic incentives to behave otherwise. To put it most simply, if it was in the interest of the owners for the CEO to shut down the company and put himself out of a job, what CEO in his right mind would do that?

It wasn't enough just to argue, as Friedman had, that it was executives' job to maximize profits. You had to address the reality that they might not want to do so. Or that, even if they did, there remained the question of which profits: This year's? Next year's? Those fifteen years down the road?

Jensen and Meckling looked to the efficient market for help. Weighing future versus present profits was one of the main things the stock market did. And by monitoring the behavior of agents and punishing value destroyers with lower share prices, financial markets provided an element of discipline that was otherwise lacking.

Figuring out how to get executives to pay attention to this verdict of the market became the focus of Jensen's career. He moved on to Harvard Business School, where he became the most prominent academic advocate of leveraged buyouts (what we now call private equity), because high indebtedness was supposed to force executives to focus on what mattered. And a few years later he became the most prominent advocate of linking executive pay to stock performance, because that was supposed to compel executives to focus on what mattered.

Without this kind of single-minded focus, the argument went, executives would be tempted to steer resources in directions that benefited chiefly themselves. You don't have to share Jensen's enthusiasm for financial markets to acknowledge that there's at least something to this: As Larry Summers wrote here before, "Inherent in the multiple objectives urged for creative capitalists is a loss of accountability with respect to performance."

But as Jensen's approach rose to dominance in the 1990s under the slogan "shareholder value," it became clear that relying on the stock market to enforce accountability was not the complete answer either. Stock prices are subject to mood swings and occasional manipulation, rendering them a less-than-perfect measure of corporate success. Executives out to maximize their stock price can and have destroyed their companies in the process.

Jensen now acknowledges this and is trying to incorporate what he calls integrity into his concept of how organizations ought to work. Other people have different ideas. But it seems to me that any discussion of the purpose of corporations needs to address the vexing dilemma that:

1. Having multiple organizational goals can be a recipe for underperformance and waste,

but

2. Focusing exclusively on a single, simple goal like profit maximization or shareholder value can lead an organization terribly astray.

A BRIEF DETOUR ON EFFICIENT MARKETS

An email exchange between Kinsley and Summers

(I emailed Justin Fox after receiving the above post, mainly to thank him, and cc'd several other participants, hoping to goad them into reaction. Only one was goaded.)

FROM MICHAEL KINSLEY:

Justin—Thanks for this interesting piece. For what it's worth, here's a bit of a reaction. The efficient markets thesis. I buy it, up to a point. Markets aren't perfectly efficient (thus, Warren Buffett), but they are more efficient than I am. Therefore, I don't play the market. Here's something I don't understand (and would love to read a piece about it someday). Even if markets *are* perfectly efficient and the price at any moment perfectly reflects all available information and wisdom about the company, there are lots of people out there trading on the basis of less-than-perfect information, or none at all, or superstitions or tips, or whatever. The efficient markets thesis tells us these people will lose money (or rather, will do worse than people who are willing to settle for doing as well as the market as a whole, which we are advised to do by investing in index funds and so on). What happens to this money they lose? Isn't there a zero-sum game here? For every person doing worse than the overall market, isn't there someone doing better? I.e., can't Warren Buffet beat the market even if the market is efficient?

Here is a puzzle. It seems intuitively correct to me that I am not smart or knowledgeable enough to beat the market. But say I started out with a million dollars and my object was to try to lose it all. And only by buying and selling shares of stocks. No fancy derivatives, no selling short. And no broker's fees. Even so, losing money playing the stock market intuitively seems like it ought to be easy. Yet if the efficient markets thesis is correct, it must be just as hard to lose a million dollars as it is to make a million dollars.

The idea that individual investors can't beat the market is called the "efficient markets thesis," but the general notion that investment markets are efficient has another half, which is the idea that publicly traded corporations run by hired-gun executives are efficient allocators and managers of capital. LBOs, private equity, and so on are a specific refutation of this second notion. Yet the retirement and pension funds of ordinary citizens are still overwhelmingly invested in the stock market, and you can go to the NYSE or NASDAQ websites and read all sorts of apparent bullshit about what a wonderful arrangement this is. So if stock markets can't set the correct price, why should they continue to exist? And what is the correct—"efficient"— price for a share of Yahoo!? Is it what a share was trading for a few months ago? What Microsoft is willing to pay, or what? Two famous economists have died in the last few years: Galbraith and Friedman. Friedman got all the glory, Galbraith was generally mocked. But didn't he get this right?

I guess we are wandering a bit far afield from creative capitalism. Thanks again for your piece.

FROM LAWRENCE SUMMERS:

Mike—I am largely untroubled by your questions. I don't think you could figure out how to systematically underperform in the stock market precisely because if you could, you could also figure out how to outperform in it. What you would do, by the way—selling stocks that look overvalued—would have caused you to sell Google at 100 and the Nasdaq in 1998 at 3,000. Nor is it clear that goofy people should lose money in a competitive market. This is one of its glories. As long as there are a reasonable number of shoppers for books, I can walk into a bookstore and, without comparison shopping, not worry too much about overpaying. Or think about the football pools. As long as there are smart guys who enter the pool when the odds wander from where they should be, stupid people won't (unless they are systematic) manage to lose more than the regular vigorish.

Whether the market is efficient is orthogonal to whether agency problems are serious. My yard is worth more to me than it would be to someone else, given where my house is. Likewise, the value of Yahoo! to Microsoft may be different from that on the public market.

Galbraith thought that large companies, typified by the auto industry, could manipulate demand to ensure they always did well. I don't think his views look good today. As for Friedman—I'm not so sure he looks bad. What is most screwed up today? GSEs, Citibank, regional banks. What is most regulated? Same list. What is least screwed up? Hedge funds and the like. What is least regulated?

If regulation means the kind of jihad against short selling that the Securities and Exchange Commission is engaged in, then God help us all.

WHAT MAKES CREATIVE CAPITALISM HARD?

Esther Duflo

In many cases, recognition—the main driving force behind creative capitalism—requires no sacrifice. Firms spend large amounts of money sponsoring things like car races to gain brand recognition, presumably because it makes economic sense. One can imagine that being associated with a sufficiently sexy philanthropic cause could be just as effective a way to advertise. I once heard the CEO of TNT, a Dutch transport and logistics company, make this argument very cogently. In explaining why he had decided to stop sponsoring Formula One rallies and instead spend money helping the World Food Programme, he argued that helping the WFP transport food in TNT trucks would do more to establish his brand as capable of rising to complex challenges than would tacking a banner to the side of a racing track. This example also underscores another reason to favor creative capitalism: We want to lure the successful entrepreneurs to the development business so that they will bring their business acumen, technical expertise, and creativity to the problems at hand—all of which are badly needed.

For these reasons, I largely share the optimism evident in Bill Gates's speech. Corporations have a unique role to play in producing good things for the world's poor, and harnessing their power, with public recognition as the currency, seems like the way to go. There is, however, a fundamental difference between producing goods or services to sell on the market and producing them to improve the lives of the poor—a difference that creates a fundamental difficulty for creative capitalism.

In their day jobs, capitalists make money and stay in business only because consumers like their products enough to pay a price high enough to allow the capitalist to make money. This ensures that businesses add value on a sustained basis. But this automatic feedback loop is generally missing in the social sector, precisely because the social sector intervenes in places where the market, left to its own devices, did not or cannot arrive at the desired outcome. In many cases, we want to deliver goods or services to people who are unable or unwilling to pay the full price: We may want to subsidize parents to have their children immunized, to have them sleep under bed nets, or to have them go to school. These cases suggest that the beneficiaries may be happy to consume certain services, even if the services are not worth their marginal costs, and especially if the alternatives are limited. But because there is no pure market test for these subsidized services, we have no pure guarantee that we are delivering something truly valuable or doing so efficiently.

The insight of creative capitalism is that the warm glow of recognition can be marketed. But the warm glow runs the risk of being divorced from any actual benefit. The altruistic motives that make a consumer, employee, or shareholder feel good are not necessarily what will help a poor person. It is in this wedge that Bill Easterly's criticism lives; in fact, he often argues that the feel-good altruism of the rich actually hurts the poor.

If creative capitalism is to fulfill its potential, it has to resolve this tension between motive and impact. It is important that the benefits of recognition be as closely aligned as possible with the creation of social value. One approach, championed by such creative capitalists as the Acumen Fund, has been to focus on identifying areas where a gap between private and social value does not exist or is small. There are many cases where the poor would be willing to pay full price for a service, but no one may have offered it yet, or there might be a way to offer it more cheaply or more effectively. Creative capitalists can focus their efforts on offering these types of services. After all, inventing new products and ways to sell them is what capitalists are good at.

These for-profit efforts should be the first way forward: By requiring that creative-capitalist ventures at least break even after some initial time, we can introduce the feedback loop normally missing from the social sector.

But it would be a shame if creative capitalists were to focus only on this sort of venture. There are many cases of goods with social benefits that the poor may not want to purchase at full price. Public health interventions are an obvious example: when there are large positive externalities—as Michael Kremer has pointed out, everyone in a community benefits from an individual vaccination—the private value is lower than the social value. As a result, requiring "sustainability" in the narrow financial sense (each project must generate enough revenue to finance itself) may result in very valuable projects not coming to fruition.

Take the example of water and sanitation. The latest fashion is to ask poor households to finance water and sanitation infrastructure via microcredit loans. But if one household refuses to be connected, the entire system may be at risk of contamination, rendering the sanitation investment useless. Thus, it makes economic sense to subsidize poor households to join. Indeed, the savings—in terms of lower government health expenditures—may be much larger than the costs, even if they don't directly accrue to the households. (And of course, there are also cases where helping the poor survive is a basic moral duty, like the refugee camps to which TNT trucks bring the WFP food.)

These examples suggest that creative capitalism should not be equated with having a "double bottom line." Plenty of worthwhile social investments may never yield a profit but will yield tremendous social returns.

This brings us back to the problem of aligning public recognition and social value.

There is a solution: Create a system in which companies have an incentive to rigorously assess the impact of the projects they support or initiate, and publish these assessments.

We now know a lot about what makes for a good or bad initiative. At MIT's Jameel Poverty Action Lab we believe that randomized evaluation, whenever possible, is the most robust way to evaluate a project. We also know more than before (though by no means nearly enough) about what works and what does not.

I would suggest two avenues for creative capitalism. The first is to focus on creative experimentation: coming up with new ideas and then spending the time and money to rigorously evaluate them, publish the results, and then move on to something else if the idea is a complete failure. A key strength of American capitalism is that failure in one enterprise does not discourage entrepreneurs or investors. It should be no different in the social sector: Failures that are analyzed and understood are as valuable as successes. This would be akin to social sector R&D.

The second avenue is scaling up: We must carry out on a large scale ideas that have been shown to work elsewhere. In choosing projects, agencies and corporations could draw on a database of failures and successes generated by others.

This will require institutions to gather, validate, and spread knowledge, and it requires some standard for what constitutes an acceptable evaluation. Enforcing this norm will not be easy. If recognition is valuable, firms will have an incentive to get more of it than they deserve. This problem is a lot like the perpetual difficulty of getting capitalist firms to present reliable and independent audits of their accounts. But it is also where the big foundations have a key role to play: They can be the ones that set the example, by setting and enforcing high standards of evaluation and transparency. The Gates and Hewlett foundations have set up an excellent example of what a reliable evaluation process could look like with their joint education initiative. Based on rigorous evaluation, they have funded projects that had shown promise and dropped ones that didn't.

DOES BEING RECOGNIZED AS A
GOOD CITIZEN MAKE A DIFFERENCE?

Tim Harford

According to Bill Gates, there are three main ways in which market incentives might be used to serve the poor. The first is that corporations should just get smarter at finding profit opportunities "at the bottom of the pyramid." There's no harm in that, but as Michael Kinsley and Warren Buffett point out in their discussion, we'd expect most of the available market opportunities to be filled already.

A second is that governments should take a role in providing incentives to help the poor. One direct way to do that is to establish prizes or quasi-prizes for companies that develop vaccines for diseases of the poor. Another is to use aid money to purchase services for the poor—so-called output-based aid. There are other possibilities too, although the example Gates gives, of rewarding philanthropic pharmaceutical firms with priority drug approval on another product, raises more questions about the waste involved in the U.S. drug approval system than about creative capitalism.

But Gates put most emphasis on a third option: using "recognition" as a "market-based incentive." I think that's worth examining closely. Many contributors have argued about whether it's legitimate for a company's managers to divert resources to social ends—with Steven Landsburg, and the spirit of Milton Friedman, at the heart of the debate. But there's another question here: Would this work? Will the quest for a good corporate name actually promote the behavior we'd like to see?

I am not sure. Think about how the quest for recognition might work as a "market-based incentive." Corporations would hope that by doing good things, or avoiding bad behavior, they'd win loyalty from employees, business from customers and suppliers, or cheaper funding from socially responsible investors. If the cost of doing the right thing is less than the reputational benefit, well, that's a successful market-based incentive to be a good corporate citizen.

Great. But under what circumstances would it work?

First, firms must be long lasting and patient enough to make the investment in good behavior up front, in anticipation of a reputational reward.

Second, the rewards for good behavior or punishments for bad behavior must be easy to inflict. It is easy to boycott a particular brand of gasoline or to buy a cool RED product. It is a bigger deal to resign from a company on ethical grounds.

Third, it must be easy to spot good behavior and bad behavior. Firms must realize that their actions really will have consequences for their reputations—consequences that can't be duplicated with a nice advertising campaign.

Fourth, the company's potential reputation must be worth more than the expense of doing the right thing.

Recognition works as a market-based incentive when these

four conditions are met, and I'm just not convinced that that will happen very often.

Think about successful reputational campaigns, and you start to realize how exceptional they are. After a lot of bad publicity about sweatshops, Nike is now regarded by many as a leader on labor standards. But Nike, which is basically a marketing outfit, finds it fairly inexpensive to respect these standards and very beneficial to do so. What have less prominent sportswear brands been doing? Who cares? Nike put resources into setting up collaborative bodies for responsible behavior, but many less prominent competitors simply declined to join. The "recognition" incentive was a success only in a very narrow way.

Product RED is a terrific idea, but again, cheap to implement and reliant on a few very brand-conscious firms, for which recognition is very important.

Contrast such efforts with the mid-1990s campaign to get Shell out of Nigeria, then run by the dictator Sani Abacha. Shell cares about recognition, for sure, but no reputational damage was ever likely to outweigh the cost of halting oil production in Nigeria. It is no surprise that Shell stayed and took the bad publicity on the chin.

Other companies that produce commodities, intermediate goods, or nonbranded products—memory chips, copper, rice—are unlikely to be seriously affected by reputational concerns.

My final worry about recognition is that we do not always recognize behavior that will truly help the poor. A simple example: A friend of mine recently bought shoes made in Italy rather than shoes made in Romania, specifically because she was worried (in a rather vague way) about encouraging sweatshop labor. That's a valid concern but clumsily expressed. I worry that most of us, being simple human beings, will also clumsily express our desires to make the world a better place, as shareholders, customers, or employees. If I'm right, recognition will be an even blunter tool.

I share with Bill Gates the conviction that capitalism has a huge role to play in helping the poor. But I am not convinced that the recognition mechanism is what will make that happen.

FOUNDATIONS COULD USE
THE KICK OF CREATIVE CAPITALISM

Alexander Friedman

Creative capitalism is mostly about reforming the way businesses work. But since much of the discussion so far has involved the role of government, I would like to point out that creative-capitalist thinking can help private foundations achieve their goals as well.

Typically, foundations separate the management of their funds from the operation of their programs. By law, they must pay out about 5 percent of their assets every year. So they invest relatively conservatively in the hope of being able to pay out that 5 percent forever, and their investment decisions are largely made without consideration of their own formal policy goals.

But foundations could invest part of their money differently, with very little risk to themselves and substantial benefit for the world's poorest people and countries. They could show how profits can be made in places where private capital currently won't invest. In short, foundations can be guinea pigs for creative capitalism.

One example of what I have in mind would likely not even require a foundation to use any actual cash, though it would provide more funds for the beneficiary than the typical foundation grant. Consider charter schools. When a public school district issues bonds to finance construction (or, for that matter, when you take out a mortgage to buy a house), the term is typically twenty or thirty years. And it is quite reasonable for a bank or other private investor to loan you money for so long with a building to back it up. But most charter schools must have their charters renewed every five years. Financial institutions are understandably reluctant to underwrite bonds for thirty years to an entity that could be out of business in five.

So some foundations are now stepping in to guarantee part of an investor's principal. This reduces the risk and makes the bonds easier to sell. And it requires no cash from the foundation at first, and probably none at all. Meanwhile, if the foundations encounter no problems, and if charter schools have little or no trouble renewing their charters, private markets could begin to handle the financing of charter schools without further assistance.

This same model could be used on a larger scale to help entire nations gain access to the capital markets. Right now, private markets may well be misreading history and treating investments in poor countries as more risky than they really are. For example, suppose a certain sub-Saharan African country cannot issue sovereign bonds because of past problems but has a new and stable government and improved economic conditions. A foundation, or group of foundations, could potentially solve that problem by agreeing to guarantee part of the bonds.

The particular purpose of the bonds ought to serve the goals of the foundations, of course. But if the nation pays back its lenders with no problems, capital markets will reassess the risk of investing there, which will be a bigger boost to the nation than almost any imaginable grant. And it won't have cost the foundation a nickel. Of course, the foundation will have to reflect the guarantee in its books. If, for example, the bond issuance was $1 billion, the guarantee was 30 cents on the dollar, and the risk of default was 50 percent, the foundation would need to record a reserve against losses of $150 million. But even so, what a bargain! For a theoretical $150 million it may never have to pay, the foundation will have unlocked a billion dollars of capital to benefit a poor nation and set up an example that private capital may wish to emulate.

Foundation aid to sovereign nations might even emulate microlending, the currently fashionable practice in which tiny business loans are made to groups of people in poor countries with inadequate financial institutions. The entire group guarantees repayment of the individual loans and becomes an effective monitor and enforcer. By the same token, suppose foundation capital were available only to groups of countries, in blocks of two or three, and that these countries were forced to monitor one another and design safeguards that satisfied one another's perceptions of mutual risk. In theory, this kind of cooperation could serve to deepen relationships between nations, with side benefits such as encouraging regional trade.

But foundations could do more to help. Undeveloped financial systems in developing countries create a chicken-and-egg problem. Potential investors usually don't know enough about the local economy to invest sensibly. The government and the local culture may not encourage entrepreneurial activity. There aren't enough trained managers or institutions to train more. The local investment banking industry may be primitive or worse. Confidence in the stability of the government may be small. All of these factors discourage outside investment, and the absence of outside investment exacerbates these problems.

So here's a suggestion: Foundations and traditional private capital could make investments in poor countries together. The foundations would agree to accept a lower-than-market rate of return so that the private investors would be willing to join in. At some point, when the investment has become profitable, the foundation would reclaim at least part of the return it has forgone. And, as with the other examples, this is not just a way to finance particular projects but a way to demonstrate to private capital that investments in developing countries can pay off. If it worked, the foundation's role could fade away.

There are variations on this model, in which foundations participate in limited partnerships with private investors or in which foundations become the buyer of last resort for investments in poor countries. But the principle in all cases is the same: The foundation can use investments to advance its program goals directly, rather than keeping the investment function and the program function apart.

As for just the foundation's program side, it can generate value on its own—intellectual property in particular—and treat it as such. For example, consider a foundation devoted to developing drugs for diseases that affect mainly poor people and countries. The obvious examples of this are efforts in AIDS, malaria, TB, and certain neglected tropical diseases. The five largest global foundations working in this area have more than 130 new drugs under development. We know what it costs to develop new drugs, and developing more than one hundred of them will cost more than any foundation, or all of them, can afford. Using traditional market forces—creative capitalism—is essential. And, with a slight shift in thinking, it should be eminently doable.

Foundations should follow the approach to intellectual property used by universities. They should analyze their programs and grants and determine where they own intellectual property, either outright or in partnership with other organizations. They should then ask where there might be commercial opportunities apart from the purpose of the original grant.

For example, a foundation may have invested large amounts of capital in a program to develop a new TB vaccine and now may have multiple candidates in phase II clinical trials. While the foundation's goal is to develop a new TB vaccine that will work under the conditions of the developing world, there may be a market for this product in the developed world as well (immigrants, health care workers, soldiers, et cetera). The foundation could sell developed-world rights to industry participants such as pharmaceutical or biotech companies, or to private equity investors. Or a bundle of these rights could be turned over to a new company that could go public or sell equity to private investors. Whatever. But the key is that proceeds to the foundation could be used to offset the development costs.

What unites all these examples is the idea that foundation capital can be more flexible than traditional private capital and can show how profits can be made in places where private capital currently won't invest. The moral is that foundations can serve their stated goals through their investments as well as through their grants—and their grants can partly repay themselves if they are thought of more like traditional investments. All it requires is a bit more creativity and a bit more capitalism.

A Reply to Alexander Friedman:
THERE'S NO SUCH THING AS A FREE LUNCH
Steven Landsburg

It is useful to talk about how foundations can best spend their resources. But it does no good at all to pretend there's such a thing as a free lunch. Alex, you talk about $150 million a foundation may never have to pay, but on average it will have to pay $150 million. Sometimes it will pay zero; sometimes it will pay $300 million; sometimes it will pay more. The reason the $150 million is on the books is because it's a reasonable expectation of the cost for your hypothetical program.

The question then becomes, Is this or is this not the best use of this $150 million? That, of course, depends on specifics that aren't addressed here. But I read the thrust of this post as saying that the foundation should creatively look for ways to spend $150 million without actually spending $150 million. There are no such ways.

PROVE THAT IT WORKS, AND IT WILL CATCH ON

Clive Crook

The most frustrating thing about the debate Bill Gates has started is that the term "creative capitalism" is so vague. It covers so many different sorts of activity that it resists a simple up-or-down vote. Rather than yielding to the temptation to come out for or against Bill's claims about creative capitalism, it might be more productive to make a few distinctions among the different ways the idea could be put into practice, sometimes with good results, sometimes not so good.

Let's start with the best and least troublesome case. Advocates of creative capitalism (previously known as corporate social responsibility) have usually insisted that it ultimately serves both shareholders and society at large. As we have seen, many economists, following Milton Friedman, are skeptical about this because if CC is profit promoting, it ought to be happening already. If it makes money, there should be no need for visionary exhortation about the social benefits, never mind calls for an entirely new kind of capitalism. My instincts put me firmly in the skeptics' camp.

Of course, this response is a variant of the "dollar on the sidewalk" argument. The point of that joke is that you do sometimes find a dollar on the sidewalk. Maybe the CC way of thinking will improve our vision (consider the longer term) or suggest new places to look (treat your staff well; listen to your customers; don't forget the bottom billion). Perhaps Bill has mostly this in mind, so far as ordinary for-profit companies are concerned. If so, the Davos stuff about a new kind of capitalism marrying sentiment and self-interest is beside the point. Forget all that: CC is just a way of making businesses better at what they already do.

Fine. I'm all for it. I will only say that when it comes to win-win CC, actions speak louder than words. Business leaders, as opposed to management gurus, have capital and other resources at their disposal. The best way for them to alert the world to missed opportunities for making money while doing good is to get on with it. Show that treating your staff well or reducing your carbon footprint pays for itself in better performance; or that fortunes can be made from meeting the needs of consumers in the developing world; or whatever. Prove it, and the idea will catch on fast.

This kind of win-win creative capitalism, however, cannot be all of what Bill has in mind, because he also says (incorrectly, in my view) that there is no money in serving the poor. Indeed, he says this is the fundamental flaw of ordinary capitalism. He therefore seems to be urging firms to sacrifice some profit in order to do good works. At this point he gets vague. It is unclear whether this selflessness will get a commercial reward later, in which case the fundamental flaw disappears, or whether it represents a permanent loss of profits. If the latter, of course, it is a kind of corporate philanthropy.

Corporate philanthropy—from your dividend to his favorite charity—is partly an issue of business ethics and corporate governance. If managers have the explicit consent (or, arguably, the tacit consent) of the firm's owners to such donations, well and good. Firms such as Whole Foods that gave a share of profits to charity when they were private companies, and then went public on the understanding that the practice would continue, are not cheating anybody. But if I saw that the music-loving CEO of a tubing manufacturer whose shares I own had chosen to sponsor an opera company, I would wish I had been asked first. And let's not be too quick to say, if shareholders don't like it, they can sell—unless we also regard that as an adequate response to other instances of managerial abuse, over insider trading, for instance, or executive pay.

In addition to win-win and what I would call borrowed virtue, two other possibilities fill out the matrix. Some CC initiatives might raise profits but inadvertently reduce welfare. Others might hurt the bottom line and set back social welfare as well.

Are there really instances of what I would call delusional CC—initiatives that lower both profits and social welfare? Absolutely. In Europe more than in the U.S., corporate social responsibility has become the corporate equivalent of political correctness. It seems to inspire a good deal of window dressing and bureaucratic overhead, to little or no economic purpose. The recycling fetish is a notable instance. Much of this is pure waste, so to speak, an outlay of effort and other resources that subtracts both from profits and from welfare. I find that many CEOs are privately willing to admit that this kind of social work is something they have to do, even though they believe it is pointless. Anything for a quiet life, is their view: They are content so long as the cost is kept low. Advocates of CC should reflect on whether they want to add to the pressure on companies to get with the program.

But it is the fourth and final category—pernicious CC—that deserves the closest attention, in my view, and that should give advocates of CC most pause. The political demands that corporations nowadays have to face may be well intentioned, but from a global welfare point of view, they are not always well judged. Big, conspicuous American and European companies face pressure to reduce offshoring of jobs, for instance, or to enforce demanding labor and environmental standards on their developing-country suppliers. Acceding to these demands may often be profit maximizing, because their businesses will suffer the disapproval of consumers otherwise. But at the very least it is an open question whether curbing investment in poor countries serves the interests of the world's poor.

Today in the U.S. we see a powerful upsurge of antitrade and antibusiness sentiment. Businesses have to navigate this as best they can. A commitment to good corporate citizenship, possibly even a genuine one, may be part of the right pragmatic response. But if it accommodates critics of capitalism by meeting them halfway, rather than facing them honestly and answering their arguments, this strategy will be partly self-defeating. If you take the view, as I do, that competition and free enterprise are engines of social progress and that there is no need to take this system back to the drawing board, you should think twice about conceding points to its opponents.

GATES FOUNDATION TO THE RESCUE!

Tracy Williams, Michael Deich, and Josh Daniel

We work at the foundation and have been thinking about creative capitalism since Bill started talking about the subject. We've spoken a bit with Bill about these issues. While we believe this note is roughly in line with his thinking, he hasn't seen it, didn't approve it, and very well might disagree with some of the specific claims it makes. We're confident, however, that Bill shares our hope that this debate about creative capitalism will encourage more businesses to consider anew the various ways in which serving the poor could also serve their interests.

What is creative capitalism?

Much of the debate here has centered on what, exactly, creative capitalism is. Here's our thinking.

• This isn't about changing capitalism, which has worked wonders for billions of people and will continue to do so. Yet roughly one billion people still make under $1 a day, about half of the people in the developing world lack access to basic sanitation, and one child dies every thirty seconds from malaria, a preventable disease. Market reforms and the spread of capitalism will help to address these problems over time. Creative capitalism seeks to harness capitalism in ways that speed this progress.

• Creative capitalism is an effort to get more companies involved in work that reduces inequity. It assumes that companies don't do more of this kind of work today because they don't face the right incentives: because they don't see how to make a direct profit from it or how to enhance the value of the business more generally from doing it. Creative capitalism is about discovering these incentives where they already exist and about creating more incentives when the current ones are insufficient.

• This can happen in two ways:
   1. Businesses can seek more effective ways to use existing market incentives—such as profit or recognition—to reduce inequities and serve the poor.
   2. Governments, nonprofits, and philanthropies can use their resources and expertise to create new market incentives for businesses to reduce inequities and serve the poor.

• Businesses can take advantage of existing market incentives to serve the poor in two general ways:
   1. Tapping profitable but previously unrecognized markets that serve the poor. As C. K. Prahalad argues in his book *The Fortune at the Bottom of the Pyramid*, businesses sometimes fail to innovate appropriately for the specific needs of these markets.

2. Supporting a social cause. By supporting a social cause, a business can enhance its reputation for "good works" and/or differentiate its product (e.g., "fair trade" coffee), thereby gaining certain customers and employees. An example is the RED campaign, where companies like Gap, Hallmark, and Dell sell RED-branded products and donate a portion of their profits to fight AIDS.

• Governments, nonprofits, and philanthropies can devise new market incentives to promote business activity that improves the lives of the poor:

1. Governments can develop legal/regulatory policies that promote creative capitalism. For example, governments can strengthen business environments generally (e.g., more clearly define and protect property rights), change trade rules (e.g., provide better market access for developing-world producers), and create specific incentives for businesses to serve the poor (e.g., the FDA priority review voucher, which Bill mentioned in his Davos speech). Ideally, such policies would specifically benefit the poor, be politically and economically sustainable, and be efficient. (Others on this blog have noted that the FDA priority review—like most policies—is not optimally efficient. We welcome and encourage efforts to make priority review and other policies as effective as possible in providing real incentives to private companies to develop medicines to treat diseases of the poor.)

2. Governments, philanthropies, and nonprofits can use their financial resources and/or technical expertise to promote business activity that benefits the poor. In some cases, short-term investments will lead to business activity that not only serves the poor but also is sustainable by markets in the long run. For example, investments in infrastructure or capacity building can enable small-holder farmers to reach broader markets and develop sustainable business models. The nonprofit TechnoServe is currently working with African coffee farmers to do just this, using a grant from the Bill & Melinda Gates Foundation. In other cases, short-term incentives for businesses can provide crucial breakthroughs in innovation to serve the poor. Advanced market commitments are an example of an initiative that uses donor funding to give businesses an incentive to produce drugs targeting developing-world diseases.

• We still have a lot to learn about creative capitalism. Creative capitalism isn't brand new, but it is happening faster and more visibly today than ever before. Real-world examples are providing a steady stream of learning opportunities, new ideas, and experienced partners. We hope that a lot more of it can happen, and in more industries, than is happening now.

Can creative capitalism be profitable?

We believe that businesses generally should view creative capitalism as a way to enhance their long-term profitability. The only exception to this would be when business owners deliberately choose to use their business as a vehicle for channeling their altruism (as we describe in the next section). The posts on this site have considered a number of ways in which business might profit through creative capitalism:

• Serving the bottom of the pyramid. As discussed above, businesses could find new markets to serve the "bottom of the pyramid." Some have argued that there can't be many opportunities to profitably serve those making under $2 a day—if such opportunities existed, businesses would already be in those markets. But information isn't perfect and markets aren't perfectly competitive, so it's reasonable to ask whether there remain significant untapped markets that would serve the poor. As C. K. Prahalad has pointed out, information gaps and misperceptions can cause businesses to neglect profitable opportunities. Pending better empirical evidence, there is every reason to encourage businesses to seek out these kind of opportunities in a more deliberate and creative fashion.

• Using "good works" to attract employees and customers. Having a reputation for pursuing actions that support the poor can help a business with its employees (by making it easier to attract and retain good people), its customers (some of whom will consider a firm's reputation when they make purchasing decisions), and other stakeholders. To the extent that reputation lowers the costs of hiring and retaining employees or increases the consumer base, it directly translates into profits.

• Corporate social responsibility (CSR). In our view, corporate social responsibility can be considered a form of creative capitalism when its purpose is to reduce inequities and when it benefits the business. The degree to which CSR is profitable depends on how it is structured. In "Strategy & Society: The Link Between Competitive Advantage and Corporate Social Responsibility" (*Harvard Business Review,* 2006), Michael Porter and Mark Kramer call on firms to practice "strategic" CSR and incorporate social factors into business strategy as a way of enhancing the firm's competitive advantage.

As noted above, creative capitalism doesn't rely on businesses alone. It also calls on governments, philanthropies, and nonprofits to consider ways that they might facilitate new and sustainable opportunities for businesses to profitably serve the poor.

Why should businesses be involved in social issues?

Another way of asking this question is "Why shouldn't companies just try to maximize profits and let their shareholders donate the cash as they see fit?" In some cases, a strict division between the pursuit of profit and the pursuit of social ends in fact will be the best approach. In other cases, however, we believe a business's expertise, products, or processes can make it the most efficient provider of a particular social benefit. For example, no one would be surprised if a pharmaceutical company were found to be an effective and efficient developer of vaccines. Thus, it makes sense that employees, consumers, and shareholders would sometimes choose to channel their altruism through a firm. For example:

- A scientist with knowledge that could benefit the poor may find it more effective to channel her altruism through her business rather than by working alone or writing a check.

- A consumer who wants to support farmers in the developing world might find that buying fair-trade products is the best way to use her resources to support that goal.

Like consumers and employees, business owners sometimes will choose to give through their firms. For example, they may set up a "social business," defined by Muhammad Yunus as an entity that seeks to maximize social goals, such as supporting the poor, while recovering its costs through market activities and reinvesting rather than distributing any profits (see Yunus's book *Creating a World Without Poverty: Social Business and the Future of Capitalism*). Another example is the low-profit limited liability company, or L3C, which is a for-profit legal entity with the explicit purpose of engaging in socially beneficial activities. The "B corporation" is another experimental business form that tries to incorporate social goals directly into the business charter. Businesses obviously need to make profits to survive in the marketplace, and they will always have a fiduciary duty to their shareholders—creative capitalism won't change that. But shareholders can and sometimes will deliberately choose to use their businesses to serve their altruistic aims.

How can we make sure that creative capitalism is effective?

We believe that creative capitalism should be accompanied by some assessment of its social impact, both to ensure that the concept is meaningful and to give effective creative capitalists legitimate credentials for their good works (and help them reap the associated reputational benefits). To this end, governments, nonprofits, and philanthropies can help in identifying and measuring the social impact of business activity, contributing to a "supporting infrastructure" for creative capitalism. For example:

• Social labels, like RugMark, provide standards for businesses and give consumers information about how products support social ends.

• The Access to Medicine index provides information for governments, academics, nonprofits, and the general public on how pharmaceutical firms support efforts to improve global access to medicines.

• Nonprofits can help businesses measure the social impact of their initiatives. For example, the Global Alliance for Improved Nutrition (GAIN), a nonprofit, and Johns Hopkins University are helping Danone (the dairy company) measure the nutritional impact of a joint venture with Grameen Bank in Bangladesh, which sells low-cost fortified yogurt to children. The one-year study will test the impact of the yogurt on Bangladeshi children, specifically looking at their growth, health, and cognitive development. If the results suggest that the initiative has been successful, Danone and the venture get great publicity. If the impact isn't as strong as hoped, the study will provide valuable information for improving the venture.

• Awards, such as the World Business and Development Awards (sponsored by the International Chamber of Commerce, the United Nations Development Programme, and the International Business Leaders Forum) and Fast Company's Social Capitalist Awards, evaluate business accomplishments and highlight them for the general public.

How important is creative capitalism in the fight against global poverty?

Making real progress in the fight against global poverty will require substantial improvements in governance, health, education, infrastructure, key economic sectors (particularly agriculture), and many other things. No single actor acting alone will be able to "solve" the problem. Developed countries need to support the integration of developing countries into the global economy, as well as give more and better aid to support their development. Developing countries need to adopt policies that promote markets and rule of law while also protecting their populations, especially the poor. None of this will happen quickly, and it won't be easy.

But we don't think that's any reason not to use every available tool. Creative capitalism offers the potential to bring more resources, and more sustainable resources, into the fight against global poverty.

That said, creative capitalism doesn't ask businesses to do things that others—whether governments or nonprofits—can do better. Creative capitalism shouldn't and won't replace these important actors and their services. Instead, it asks businesses to consider whether there are ways in which they can serve the poor efficiently and effectively while also serving their own interests. Not every business will be able to find a comparative advantage in such activities, and that's okay. Creative capitalism asks only that more businesses consider the question and that governments, nonprofits, and philanthropies see if they can better achieve their goals or stretch their resources by creating incentives to bring businesses into their work.

Some of the people in this debate have asked whether creative capitalism is really any different from traditional capitalism. If businesses are just using their natural incentives, then what is there to call for? Won't businesses pursue creative capitalism organically, if it really is in their interests?

We think there is value in calling for creative capitalism. Firms don't have perfect information or know all of the opportunities that are out there, and fads in business strategy come and go. Moreover, governments, nonprofits, and philanthropies can create new incentives for businesses, and they can help to make creative capitalism smarter and better by tracking its social impacts. Creative capitalism is about pushing the boundary of innovation and asking all of these actors—businesses, governments, nonprofits, and philanthropies—to experiment more boldly and more deliberately, with the hope of unlocking new potential for capitalism to bring people out of poverty.

A Reply to the Foundation:
YOU'RE OUT OF TOUCH
Gregory Clark

his memo's suggestions are striking for how they touch at best tangentially on the fundamental problems of world poverty. It is aid that will at best ameliorate the symptoms of poverty, not treat its cause.

African agriculture suffers from low productivity. Africans are poorly nourished and exposed to disease. Credit institutions are weak. But the fundamental problem for Africa is none of these things. It is the failure to develop significant manufacturing and service enterprises, despite astonishingly cheap labor. Production workers in East Africa, for example, cost about $0.40 per hour compared to $10 to $20 or more in the U.S. and the European Union. Yet industrialization has escaped Africa.

The apparel industry in particular offers a path out of poverty for poor countries. Labor costs are the majority of costs. Huge markets in the EU and the U.S. are open. The average American allegedly owns eight pairs of jeans! Transport costs are fairly low. The technology is simple. Why isn't Africa a major supplier?

The poorest countries in Asia—Cambodia, Laos, and Bangladesh—are rapidly entering this industry and exporting sub-stantial quantities of garments. Yet African countries at the same income level—Tanzania, Kenya, Angola—have seen no growth in the industry.

Mauritius alone among African countries has succeeded in manufacturing apparel. Even though it is inconveniently located in the Indian Ocean (nine hundred miles east of Madagascar), has a population of only 1.2 million, and at independence in 1968 had an economy entirely based on sugar production, Mauritius has used its apparel industry to join the middle-income ranks. Its 1.2 million people, mainly the descendants of indentured plantation workers imported in the colonial period from India, export more than $1,000 of apparel per person per year, even though all the ingredients for this industry have to be imported.

The international apparel industry is footloose in search of cheaper labor. Its restless entrepreneurs are similarly cosmo-politan: Chinese, Indian, and Korean. Yet so far, they see little profit in employing the cheapest workers on the planet, those of sub-Saharan Africa. But if development is to come to Africa it will be through these entrepreneurs.

Unfortunately, major U.S. corporations—which operate in a high-wage, high-education economy—have little to offer African countries that need industrialization, because these corpo-rations specialize in producing goods for which cheap labor is not essential. They have no special insight into the problem of effectively mobilizing (via productive employment) the impov-erished masses of sub-Saharan Africa.

Bill Gates has issued a call for action. But such a call as-sumes that US corporations can easily identify what actions will help end African poverty. If they turn to academic econo-mists for an answer, they will be sorely disappointed.

Another Reply to the Foundation:
WHAT ARE YOU SAYING?
Steven Landsburg

I have no idea what the authors of this memo are trying to say, and neither, I am pretty sure, do they.

First bullet point: *This isn't about changing capitalism.* Second bullet point: *Creative capitalism is an effort to get more companies involved in work that reduces inequity.* Oh—so maybe it is about changing capitalism. Firms either do or do not seek to maximize profits to the exclusion of other goals. Add more goals, and you've changed capitalism.

By way of diverting attention from this glaring inconsistency, the authors say that under CC, firms will continue to maximize profit; they'll just do a better job of it by finding new ways to serve the poor. Well, it's true that most firms have room to improve. They overlook opportunities to serve the poor, and they overlook opportunities to serve the rich. Is CC a call for more diligence about the former but not the latter? Or a call for more diligence all around?

If CC is just about diligence in the pursuit of profit, then every disgruntled shareholder at every corporate annual meeting is a creative capitalist. If it's about diligence with respect to some opportunities more than others, then it's a diversion from profit maximization.

So which is it? I can't tell, and reading the memo doesn't help. All I find are platitudes like: *Businesses can seek more effective ways to use existing market incentives . . . to reduce inequities and serve the poor.* So when firms face conflicting incentives, is this or is this not a call to weight some of those incentives disproportionately (and therefore, implicitly, to dilute the goal of profit maximization)? That's a yes-or-no question. Why isn't it answered here? It looks like the authors want to pretend that the answer is both yes and no.

And on and on it goes. Businesses, we're told, can do all kinds of cool things, like *tapping profitable but previously unrecognized markets that serve the poor.* Well, tapping profitable but previously unrecognized markets that serve the poor can be a great strategy for profit maximization. So can tapping profitable but previously unrecognized markets that serve the rich. Being more attuned to the former than the latter means, again, diluting the goal of profit maximization. But the authors say they don't want to dilute that goal. So once again, what do they want?

Well, they want businesses to produce products that serve the poor, and they want businesses to support social causes. These, they say, are the "two general ways" for businesses to serve the poor. But this overlooks the *primary* way that businesses serve the poor: by making them more productive, or, in the vernacular, by creating jobs for them. The best thing Nike can do for third worlders is not to provide them with low-cost sneakers; it's to employ them in making high-cost sneakers for rich Westerners.

By the way: Why all the emphasis on things that corporations can start doing instead of on things corporations can stop doing? Would it be an example of CC if Archer Daniels Midland stopped lobbying for sugar quotas? We should talk about whether this sort of "negative CC" gets you more or less bang for the buck than the "positive CC" being envisioned here. My guess is that if corporations are willing to forgo profit in the pursuit of greater social good, then they can do far, far more good by laying off their demands for subsidies and protection than by anything being envisioned here.

Next, the memo asks: *Why shouldn't companies just try to maximize profits and let their shareholders donate the cash as they see fit?* A fair question. I recently had my roof redone. I could have given my roofer an extra $1,000 and instructed him to make a $1,000 charitable contribution, but that seems like a very ineffective way to be charitable. I don't want corporate executives choosing my charities any more than I want my roofer choosing my charities. Why can't shareholders simply direct the corporation to maximize profit and then contribute a share of their earnings to charity?

By way of an answer, the authors offer a total of two bulleted examples, at least one of which is patently absurd: A *consumer who wants to support farmers in the developing world might find that buying fair-trade products is the best way to . . . support that goal.*

Well, yes, I suppose that a consumer with a passionate desire to raise the wages of coffee farmers (as opposed to sugar farmers or sheepherders or urban indigents) might accomplish his goal by purchasing fair-trade coffee. But I both hope and expect that very few consumers are burdened with such a bizarrely crabbed sort of altruism.

Never mind the fact that "fair trade" seems to be a euphemism for the enforcement of monopoly power (enriching some producers by pricing others out of the marketplace); this isn't the place to get into that debate. But this much is directly to the point: Lots of people feel a moral obligation to help poor people in general. No sane person feels a moral obligation to help poor coffee farmers in particular. So the "creative capitalism" solution serves a nonexistent goal—and this was one of the best two examples the authors could come up with!

In fact, the whole fair-trade thing is an excellent illustration of creative capitalism gone insane. You can pay an inflated price for your coffee and put a farmer out of work, or you can buy ordinary coffee, contribute to CARE, and feed a starving child. Please, oh please, don't trick people into thinking the former is a good deed.

The memo concludes with *the hope of unlocking new potential for capitalism to bring people out of poverty.* This point cannot be overemphasized: Capitalism has brought most of the world out of poverty, and nothing else has ever brought any substantial number of people out of poverty. Ever. (If there's a counterexample I'm unaware of, I hope someone will tell me.)

Most of the world's poor are poor because they live under confiscatory governments. It's not enough to ask how to provide them with goods or with incomes; we've also got to ask how to prevent those goods or incomes from being confiscated. If we don't address that, I fear we'll accomplish very little. And I'm not sure I see how anything in this memo contributes to that problem.

Finally: There's been much talk here about what governments, businesses, and philanthropists can do to help. Given the contributor list on this project, it might be useful to ask what intellectuals and journalists can do. My answer: We, perhaps in conjunction with governments, businesses, and philanthropists, can remind people of where wealth comes from, of how wealth without capitalism is a fantasy, and of how this translates into concrete policy questions. Undermining the antisweatshop movement would be an excellent place to start.

LET US EXPLAIN OURSELVES

Tracy Williams, Michael Deich, and Josh Daniel

Steven Landsburg writes: "I have no idea what the authors of this memo are trying to say." We hope this note will help clear things up.

1. Landsburg argues that getting "more companies involved in work that reduces inequity" necessarily requires "changing capitalism."

We disagree. Creative capitalism is not about changing the structure of capitalism; it's about using that structure in more creative ways. It's a cell phone company that figures out how to turn low-income Africans into a market (e.g., Safaricom in Kenya); or a government that amends an outdated law to free businesses and farmers from costly middlemen (e.g., the government of Madhya Pradesh, in the case of ITC's e-Choupal initiative). These examples don't require companies to override their business priorities; they show how capitalism can be better harnessed to serve the world's poorest.

2. Landsburg writes, "If [creative capitalism is] about diligence with respect to some opportunities more than others, then it's a diversion from profit maximization."

C. K. Prahalad and others believe that rich-world firms are more likely to look for opportunities in rich-world markets than in developing-world markets. (Not that these firms are incapable of understanding markets in the developing world—but rather they haven't looked closely enough or thought creatively enough about them.) If this is true, then developing world markets may be underexploited relative to their potential, in which case firms should spend relatively more time studying the needs of developing-world markets. We don't have evidence to test this hypothesis, and the reality likely varies from firm to firm—obviously each firm needs to decide for itself whether investigating these opportunities is a worthwhile investment.

3. Landsburg writes that we overlook "the primary way that businesses serve the poor: by making them more productive."

We certainly support business efforts to provide jobs and improve livelihoods for the poor. A great creative capitalist example is Grameen Danone Foods, a partnership between Danone (a leader in the global dairy industry) and Grameen Bank to produce low-cost, nutritious yogurt for the poor in Bangladesh. The project sources milk from local producers, turns it into micronutrient-fortified yogurt, and markets the yogurt through a network of local women vendors. Danone enhances its reputation, discovers new innovations, and gains familiarity with a new market, while the venture provides jobs in the local economy and fights malnutrition.

But we question Landsburg's assumption that creating jobs is always the best thing businesses can do for the poor. For example, Landsburg writes, "The best thing Nike can do for third worlders is not to provide them with low-cost sneakers; it's to employ them in making high-cost sneakers for rich Western-ers." But what if Nike could also find a way to provide low-cost sneakers to low-income consumers? And if you replace "sneak-ers" with "vaccines" and "Nike" with "GlaxoSmithKline," the implications are even more stark—tiered pricing in that case not only taps a low-income market, but it also saves lives.

4. Landsburg writes that corporations "can do far, far more good by laying off their demands for subsidies and protection than by anything" envisioned under creative capitalism.

It would be wonderful if companies chose to forsake protec-tionism. But we are not so naïve as to think that firms will act in ways that they see as being inconsistent with their self-interest. Creative capitalism starts from a fundamentally differ-ent premise—working with the incentives faced by business to find common ground between their interests and those of the poor.

As Landsburg says, capitalism has brought many people out of poverty, and it will continue to do so. But why not ask whether we can push the boundary of capitalist innovation fur-ther and faster? We don't claim to have the answers; the people who will shape the outcomes are those from the public, private, and nonprofit sectors who heed the call for creative capitalism.

THE SEARS SOLUTION

David Vogel

More than a century ago, Sears, Roebuck's Julius Rosenwald pioneered an innovative approach to corporate philanthropy that exemplifies Gates's contemporary vision of creative capitalism. In the late nineteenth century, farmers were then among the least affluent of Americans, and American farming practices were inferior to those of western Europe. And so, shortly after purchasing Sears in 1895, Rosenwald decided to help disseminate the scientific farming knowledge and new farming skills that had been developed during the previous two decades but were still inaccessible to all but the richest and largest farmers.

His strategy was to fund county farm agents and establish a network of 4-H youth development clubs. For nearly a decade, until they were taken over the by the Department of Agriculture, these highly effective programs were supported exclusively by Sears, Roebuck. And Sears itself did well by doing good. The company's role in improving agricultural skills and farm productivity increased farm income, thus increasing the demand for Sears' products. Within a decade, a firm that had been on the verge of bankruptcy became the nation's first successful national retailer. The Sears catalogue came to occupy a prominent place, along with the Bible, in millions of American homes.

Gates is essentially challenging current corporate leaders to follow Rosenwald's inspiring example. He wants them to help improve the lives of those whom the global market economy has left behind.

This challenge raises three questions. The first is a variation on Gary Becker's: Do the constraints imposed by increased international competition and more efficient capital markets make it possible for global firms to act as responsibly as Sears did? One answer is that it might if, as Gates suggests, recognition for good works can yield benefits that translate into profits. But that suggestion raises two more questions: Can acting more responsibly actually improve a firm's bottom line? And, third, if a firm is doing good works in order to maximize profits, does it still deserve to be recognized as socially responsible?

The encouraging news is that it is possible, in response to the first question, for global firms to act more responsibly and survive in a competitive market. During the last two decades, despite heightened pressure from global competition, the number of businesses that accept the principles and practices of global corporate social responsibility (CSR) has steadily increased. Virtually every major global firm based in a developed country, as well as a growing number in developing ones, now has a program devoted to good works. Voluntary standards for corporate environmental, labor, and human rights practices now exist for scores of global industries, including clothing and athletic equipment, minerals and mining, financial services, forestry, fisheries, chemicals, toys, tourism, coffee, cocoa, palm oil, diamonds, energy, and computers and electronic equipment. Many firms have developed partnerships with international nongovernmental organizations (NGOs) to help carry out their global CSR commitments.

The UN Global Compact, the largest worldwide code of conduct for businesses, has now more than 3,500 corporate signatories, including a substantial number from developing countries. More than 2,300 firms have endorsed the International Chamber of Commerce's Business Charter for Sustainable Development. More than seventy major global financial institutions from sixteen countries, representing assets of $4.5 trillion, have adopted the UN Principles for Responsible Investment—which commit them to integrating environmental, social, and governance (ESG) issues into their investment analyses—while sixty-six financial institutions have subscribed to the Equator Principles, which have established environmental and human rights standards for project financing.

To be sure, compliance with many of these codes and standards remains uneven. But the significant and steady expansion of what has been termed "civil regulation" reflects an important change in global business norms and practices. Becker need not worry: Few if any firms have intentionally sacrificed their bottom lines in order to pursue some social goal. But when faced with pressures from NGOs and the threat of media exposés, many global firms have come to recognize that the public now holds them responsible for more than wealth creation. It also expects them to absorb and pay for the costs, such as environmental degradation, that their activities impose on others; increase the supply of public goods by, among other things, engaging in community development efforts; reduce global economic inequality by improving wages and working conditions, and in the case of pharmaceutical firms, increase global access to medical care. More than two thousand firms now publish annual reports on their domestic and international social and environmental programs, commitments, and practices, many of which are independently audited.

While we lack accurate data on how many additional resources firms have devoted to global social and environmental programs, the amount of such expenditures is far from trivial, especially if one includes the amount of time senior management spends on these issues. What we do know is that the firms that have been CSR leaders—those that make social or environmental expenditures greater than those of their competitors—have not become less competitive. There are few if any cases of the capital markets reducing a firm's value because that firm has increased its CSR expenditures or strengthened its CSR commitments.

Why is this the case? An important reason is that managers can plausibly claim that virtually any corporate expenditure on good works is in the interest of its shareholders. In many cases, such expenditures represent a form of risk management or public relations: they can improve a firm's reputation and protect the value of its brands—which gives rise to the joke that CSR stands for "corporate scandal response." In other cases, CSR expenditures have created new market opportunities, improved community relations and employee morale, and, in the case of some pollution control measures, reduced costs. These business benefits are often difficult to measure—but in that regard, CSR is no different from other kinds of expenditure, like lavish headquarters or public art displays.

The American retailer Target allocates 5 percent of its pretax earnings to community groups located near its stores. This expenditure on good works is considerably greater than those of most other corporations, including the firms with which Target competes, like Wal-Mart. In fact, the average corporate expenditure on philanthropy is currently 0.7 percent of pretax earnings. Yet Target has prospered in the highly competitive retail market, and there is no evidence that the capital markets have penalized the company for its above-average philanthropic expenditures. To the extent that financial analysts are even aware of Target's community-giving program, they presumably have deferred to the judgment of the firm's managers that these expenditures make business sense.

In a highly unusual move, Google informed its shareholders in its initial public offering that its business objectives would not be confined to maximizing shareholder value. And in fact, Google has allocated significant funds to both corporate philanthropy and some highly risky investments in alternative energy. Yet Google's IPO was extremely successful and its shares have remained relatively highly valued. The reason is straightforward: All the capital markets care about is its strong growth prospects.

So the good news is that the financial markets do not necessarily penalize more responsible firms. The disappointing news is that they don't necessarily reward them, either. The claim that CSR makes firms more profitable is endlessly repeated in books and articles and classrooms, and is believed by many business students. It also underlies the business rationale for both social investment funds and the large CSR consulting industry. However, a recent comprehensive review of 166 academic studies conclude that the impact of CSR on corporate financial performance is positive, but only very slightly. In short, CSR appears to have little impact on corporate competitiveness.

One can certainly cite examples of financially successful

firms, such as Whole Foods and Patagonia, for which CSR has been a critical part of their business strategy. Other firms such as Unilever and Nike have benefited financially from their global CSR initiatives. But there are also many examples of firms with strong global CSR records and reputations that have not performed well financially. Consider the Gap.

One of the world's largest clothing retailers, the Gap Inc. has an excellent CSR reputation. It has long been seriously committed to the welfare of the workers in its extensive supply chain in developing countries. More recently, the Gap Inc. has been a strong corporate supporter of Product RED, prominently displaying Product RED merchandise in its stores. Yet, in recent years, the Gap Inc.'s sales and earnings have been disappointing. Its strong commitment to global CSR is not the cause of these financial difficulties, but neither have Gap's sales of RED products compensated for the poor design of its stores and the current lack of fashion appeal of its clothing.

Starbucks sells fair-trade coffee and has actively worked to improve the environmental practices and earnings of the farmers from whom it purchases coffee. Yet, faced with earnings that have disappointed Wall Street, the firm recently closed six hundred stores. With consumers no longer as willing to pay almost as much for a cup of coffee as for a gallon of gas, its sales growth has slowed and it has been forced to reduce some of its prices. Did Starbucks's CSR programs, which it has prominently featured in its public relations, benefit the firm? Quite possibly, though it is unclear by how much. One suspects that few of its customers either know or care about them. In any event, Wall Street is apparently not impressed by Starbucks's good works. All the shareholders notice is the decline in its current and projected sales and earnings.

There is also a structural reason why a brand's public identification with CSR is rarely a source of competitive advantage: It can too easily be imitated by its competitors. If a firm believes that its competitors have or might gain an advantage in the marketplace though its public espousal of some CSR initiative, such as engaging in a cause-related marketing program, developing a partnership with a respected NGO, or adopting some social or environmental cause, it can rapidly and easily follow their example. In fact, virtually every consumer brand now has some CSR linkage. As a result, while many firms are now acting, or appear to be acting, more virtuously, few of them have gained a competitive advantage from doing so. Paradoxically, the more firms that do good works, the less likely it is that any particular firm will benefit from a strong CSR reputation.

Still, while there are certainly limits to how many good works a firm can do, few firms appear to have reached them. Engaging in more extensive and creative corporate philanthropy may not measurably improve a company's competitive position, but neither will it undermine it. And there is little point in disparaging a firm's good works on the grounds that they may increase, or at least are intended to increase, the firm's sales. Nothing is gained by second-guessing why managers seek to narrow the gap between corporate and public goals. What matters is what they do, not why they do it. Rosenwald still deserves to be recognized for improving the welfare of American farmers, even if his initiatives also improved Sears' bottom line. Wanting a firm to be publicly recognized for being a good citizen is as legitimate as wanting to be appreciated by investors for its steady earnings growth. Nor should Mike Kinsley worry: Few people believe that firms behave virtuously for strictly altruistic reasons.

A Reply to David Vogel:
THE DEMAND FOR VIRTUE IS RISING
Conor Clarke

David, before I read your piece, the simplified way in which I'd been dividing the world of creative capitalism (as it applies to corporations) was as follows: First, there are firms for which "recognition" is just another word for profit maximization. That is, they do good things because it gives them a happier staff, attracts more dedicated consumers, helps them disguise greed, or whatever ("public relations charity," in Posner's words). Second, there are firms for which good works do mean a real sacrifice to the bottom line. And even if these firms get some kind of recognition out of the sacrifice, it isn't recognition that translates readily into profits.

It seems to me that there is a pretty significant difference in kind between the two. The first case requires no extra justification: firms are just playing by the rules of profit maximization. (In which case one might ask: Is there anything creative about it?) But I think the second case does require some extra justification, because it raises at least two worries. The first has come up a couple of times in this discussion: If firms are going to be diverting profits for a good cause, why don't they give them out as wages and dividends and let the workers and shareholders pick their own worthy causes? The second worry is Becker's: If the firm is sacrificing profit to pursue something else, will it survive in a competitive market?

If I understand your argument correctly, you offer two reasons why Becker shouldn't worry. The first is that, as you put it, "few if any firms have intentionally sacrificed their bottom lines in order to pursue some social goal." But of course that shouldn't stop Becker from losing sleep over the firms that do sacrifice bottom line, however few and far between they happen to be. And anyway, Gates does seem to be suggesting, or at least hoping, that such firms will become more common. So I wonder if Becker's question still stands: What do you say to the managers who do declare their intentions to pursue something other than profit maximization?

I take it you'd tell them something like "don't worry too much," which is the second (and more suggestive) reason you think Becker shouldn't worry. Basically, I read your article as challenging the distinction I draw above between socially responsible firms that sacrifice profits and those that don't, because, in a nutshell, you argue that it's hard to locate a link between responsibility and profitability. Or, as you put it, "CSR appears to have little impact on corporate competitiveness."

My immediate reaction to this was that we must have a measurement problem here. Sure, maybe Target doesn't go bust giving away a pretax 5 percent, but what if it were giving away 15 percent? Or 50? At what point would the market punish managers who did this sort of thing? And isn't it conceivable that Target would be more competitive if it gave away only

3 percent or that Google's share value would be higher if it hadn't declared its do-gooder intentions at the IPO?

I suppose I had been imagining a kind of "CSR Laffer Curve": There is a point at which CSR expenditures maximize profit, beyond which the diminishing returns don't justify additional expenditures (or at least don't justify them in profit maximization terms). Even if the relationship isn't a terribly robust one, it seems as though varying CSR expenditures must affect profits at the margin—just as building a $100 million corporate headquarters must have consequences that are different from building a $1 billion one, noisiness of data aside. (This is basically a retread of the point Steven Landsburg has made several times: Even if the amount of money is small, it doesn't absolve us from asking where it comes from.)

So here's a second question: Is my distinction between the two kinds of firms above a bad one because it assumes a relationship that really doesn't exist? Or is the problem simply that it's often hard to tell the difference between firms that pursue profit maximization and firms that don't?

A final reaction. You point out that firms are signing up for all sorts of "voluntary" new international codes and charters, and you offer one interpretation of this trend: firms can give up more for the sake of CSR without being punished by investors. But I wonder if Posner or Landsburg could just as easily give this trend a different spin: The bar for disguising greed is getting higher, but the basic formula—do good works for selfish reasons—remains exactly the same.

This interpretation doesn't mean your trend is a bad one— I'm on board with your point, contra Kinsley, that we shouldn't worry too much about why corporate managers do "good things"—but, as a matter of emphasis, it does make the story more about the demand side than the supply side. (And I think you allude to this possibility.) In other words, it's not that the corporate managers of the world are becoming more virtuous but that the demand for virtue is rising and corporate managers are scrambling to respond. How does that story sound to you?

A Reply to Conor Clarke:
LET'S NOT BE TOO CYNICAL
David Vogel

Conor, I welcome the opportunity to respond to the questions you raise about my analysis.

Your distinction between firms that engage in various forms of creative capitalism in the interests of profit maximization and those whose good works represent a real sacrifice to the bottom line is an artificial one. In practice, it is virtually impossible to distinguish between the two, since I am unaware of almost any publicly traded corporation that deliberately sacrifices corporate profits in order to make the world a better place.

A more useful distinction is between firms for which various kinds of CSR have a tangible impact on the bottom line and those for which its benefits are more difficult to measure. For example, many corporate environmental expenditures have yielded important business benefits: They have created new market opportunities (such as for organic or more energy efficient products); new investment opportunities (such as alternative energy); or they have reduced the costs of packaging, transportation, or energy. Other firms have developed new markets for their products in developing countries—often associated with the needs of those at the "bottom of the pyramid." For these firms, the distinction between good works and "normal" profit maximization is often difficult to draw.

Most business activities associated with CSR do not fall into this category. They are not strategic and do not affect a firm's core business operations; rather, they are more akin to what Posner has characterized as "public relations charity." In some cases, such when the CEO makes a large donation to her husband's favorite cultural activity, they could be characterized as a form of rent. In such cases, there is an ethical case to be made that such expenditures should instead be distributed in the form of wages or dividends, thus enabling employees and shareholders to choose their own charities. However, the amount of such expenditures is rarely of sufficient magnitude that either shareholders or employees would notice them. And an important justification for corporate philanthropy is that it is much more efficient for the firm to make a substantial charitable contribution than it is for large numbers of shareholders or employees to each contribute a few additional pennies or dollars.

But typically, and increasingly, corporate good works are indirectly related to the firm's core business. Thus, firms tend to make charitable contributions and engage in other kinds of CSR expenditures in order to generate goodwill or avoid negative publicity. They focus such expenditures on public concerns that are linked to the firm's business or direct them to various constituencies that are important to the firm. Now, the claim that the magnitude and thus the social impact of such expenditures, such as those undertaken by Target, the Gap, or Starbucks, are constrained by market pressures is certainly correct.

As I argue in my book *The Market for Virtue: The Potential and Limits of Corporate Social Responsibility*, the increased competitive environment in which firms find themselves clearly limits the amount of resources they can devote to CSR. But this does not mean that it is impossible for firms to make such expenditures. Much CSR takes place at the margin. However, given the large size of many global firms, such marginal expenditures can make and often have made a discernible impact on public welfare.

To those managers who declare their intention to pursue something other than profit maximization, I would make two responses. First, in most cases I wouldn't believe them. Second, as I note above, it is possible to combine profit maximization with being a somewhat more responsible company, especially as the costs of most expenditures to further the latter objective is marginal compared to other corporate investments and expenses.

Could Target make charitable expenditures that represented 15 percent or 50 percent of its pretax earnings? Could the Gap insist that its contractors in India pay wages comparable to those in the U.S.? Could Starbucks make sure all the growers from whom it purchases coffee receive a living wage? Of course not. On the other hand, I doubt that the share prices of any of their firms would be higher if they reduced their current level of CSR expenditures. Nor do I believe that Google's share value would be higher if it had not declared its do-gooder intentions in its IPO.

My proof is straightforward: Just read the reports of share analysts. These rarely if ever warn investors to reduce their holdings in a particular firm because it is devoting too many resources to CSR. Nor do major institutional investors ever pressure firms to do fewer good works lest their shares be downgraded. The only exception I can think of is Costco. A few years ago, some analysts complained that it was mistreating its shareholders by treating its employees more generously than its competitors did. But Costco did not change its employment practices, on the grounds that they resulted in more productive employees and less shrinkage, and its share price subsequently rebounded.

But one reason why more "responsible" firms do not do better financially may, as you suggest, be linked to a measurement problem: Defining CSR is difficult. CSR is a multidimensional concept, and firms rarely act consistently across a whole range of social and environmental practices. This makes it difficult to determine the precise financial impact of any particular dimension of CSR, and it also renders suspect those rankings of the "most responsible firms" on which studies of the correlation between CSR and financial performance usually rely. No one has ever satisfactorily addressed this measurement problem, and it may well be impossible to do so—notwithstanding the claims of scores of books and hundreds of management consultants who confidently assure managers that they can "prove" how and why CSR pays.

As for your last point, about the corporations that sign on to voluntary codes: I certainly agree that many of their motivations can be questioned. Much of CSR is demand driven—or, in your words, the "bar for disguising greed has become higher." But I also think this spin does not present the whole picture. The relentless pressures for increased global CSR have affected business norms. Many managers of global firms have become more aware of the structural shortcomings of globalization. And they have responded by attempting to use some of their firms' skills and resources to address some of these short-comings—especially when they are directly linked to their firm's business operations or can be ameliorated by them. Some of these corporate programs have been highly effective. In short, we can be cynical about much of what is labeled CSR. But let's not be too cynical.

THE REAL BLIND SPOTS
OF TODAY'S CAPITALISTS

Matt Miller

I'd like to offer a closing provocation that challenges the premise of creative capitalism's proponents. Because the truth is—apart from finding new commercial opportunities, à la C. K. Prahalad—that business's greatest potential contribution to the global poor has nothing to do with how companies operate. It lies instead with the broader public policies that capitalists support or oppose.

Here's my logic (using the U.S. as an example):

1. The biggest threat to the poverty-ending power of capitalism today is the looming backlash against free trade and open markets in the developed world, especially in the U.S. If the rich world shuts its borders, we'll hurt economic prospects elsewhere in ways that no amount of "creative capitalism," as discussed here, can begin to offset.

2. The paradox, then, is that the biggest, most "creative" boost American capitalists can offer the world's poor is to ease the economic anxiety of workers here at home—because it's their insecurity that will fuel the protectionist backlash.

3. Easing this economic anxiety means providing better health care and pension security for average workers.

4. This can't happen without government playing a bigger role and supplanting over time the central (and unique) role corporations have come to play in the American welfare state. It will also entail higher taxes.

5. American capitalists—including, perhaps, Mr. Gates, though I've not seen him speak to these questions—are generally confused about the necessity of this transition. On the one hand, business leaders want to get out of the health care and pension business, because soaring costs are killing them. But in the next breath most executives say they don't want "big government" more involved. Who else do they think is available?

6. In addition, American capitalists wrongly believe that the higher taxes needed to support this transition would hurt the economy, when the evidence from other advanced nations shows that the modestly higher taxes required to relieve corporations of this burden, and plug other gaps in the safety net are perfectly consistent with strong economic growth. America would not become France or Sweden.

7. If I'm right about the above, then those who support the goals of creative capitalism might consider a different focus for their energies. Instead of challenging business to be more pseudo-altruistic in serving the world's poor, they should persuade American business leaders to move beyond antique notions about the proper role of government and the corporation in providing health and pension security, and past outdated thinking about the relationship between taxes and economic growth. These two blind spots of the planet's leading capitalists are now the biggest risk to the future of capitalism and therefore to the well-being not only of the U.S. but of billions around the globe.

THE BAD SIDE EFFECTS
OF FORCING GOOD BEHAVIOR

Edmund S. Phelps

Bill Gates's speech might give you two misimpressions. First, it seems to suggest, at least to those who go scarcely beyond the title, that capitalism won't be creative until it is reshaped as Gates proposes. But as my work for more than a decade has stressed, creativity is capitalism's essence and trump card. Capitalism, as I see it, is a system for new ideas—the inspiration, development, and ultimately the competition of ideas that their creators believe are of commercial value. Many of this system's rewards are essential elements of the Western humanist conception of the good life: the mental stimulation offered by novelty, the challenge of solving new problems, the pleasure of exploration, the thrill of discovery, the fun of originality, and the satisfaction from the advancement and personal growth that results.

The second misimpression lies in Gates's claim that "Capitalism harnesses self-interest in helpful and sustainable ways, but only on behalf of those who can pay." Gates is only half right: I would say that a country with a well-functioning market system does a world of good for the least advantaged by generating high employment and pulling up wages on every rung of the ladder. Above all, it provides meaningful careers—which communism in Eastern Europe failed to do and which corporatism in Western Europe is finding difficult to do.

But once we move beyond these misimpressions, we can consider Gates's central vision: The creative reach of a capitalist economy can and should be extended to provide vaccines, mosquito nets, and other tools for public health in poverty-stricken countries, and—most visionary—to provide new technologies particularly suited to those countries. As others have suggested here, this would mean drastically expanding something akin to "corporate social responsibility." Would it be desirable to do it, all things considered? How should we think about it?

Questions about the role of CSR inevitably raise questions about the role of altruism—questions about whether altruism is prevalent or about as real as Santa Claus; and, if prevalent, whether it is actually useful.

I hope we can agree that there are people in the world with an unselfish altruistic streak—butchers who give fair weight for money, as Adam Smith put it, and employees who put shoulder to the wheel even when an employer can't see them. There are, of course, businesspeople who seem not to have an altruistic bone in their bodies. (Perhaps they save it for home.) But we should all agree that genuine altruism does exist.

Yet standard economics—the neoclassical theories on which students must cut their teeth—sees little use for altruism, since, it's thought, incentives can be legislated to achieve the same results. Kindness on the road may save lives, but traffic laws and punishments will do the same. Charity to the poor may make everyone feel better, but redistributive taxation can do the job as well or better. Some economists conclude that economic altruism is bad or unnecessary and that "greed" is good. But that conclusion is too simplistic.

In modern economics, altruism has a potential for good. Decades ago—in 1971, at the Russell Sage Foundation—I organized a conference on the benefits from various expressions of altruism in real-life market economies, which are bedeviled by all kinds of problems stemming from the participants' imperfect information. My thought was that an altruistic spirit in a country can be—and is—drawn upon to ameliorate some of those problems. Tax cheating is a good example: Altruism toward one's fellow taxpayers on April 15 has huge social benefits. By playing it straight on our income taxes—even when the chance of fraud detection is minimal—we preserve the tax base and make possible lower tax rates for any given level of government expenditure. Everyone is better off than they would be in a Hobbesian state, in which everyone would cheat.

There are plenty of analogous situations in business. When I was a schoolkid, I was impressed by Henrik Ibsen's play *An Enemy of the People,* in which a firm does not disclose that, to keep its costs down, it produces with a method that will deplete the town's water supply. Sure, as neoclassical economics says, the town ought to have enacted a law providing penalties to deter such behavior. But maybe the firm could have escaped the penalties by consuming its capital to the point of being unable to pay them.

Some people steal time from their employer, called malingering, or steal goods from their employer, called pilfering. The typical firm sets an "incentive wage" so that employees would have "something to lose" when caught cheating and fired.

When all firms raise wages, though, no firm gets a competitive edge and the cheating is not remedied. It will lead to nothing more than higher labor prices, which leads to higher unemployment. Altruism would solve that problem: If employees recognize that when they cheat they harm one another and are conscience-stricken enough to stop cheating, wages and unemployment would fall back to where they were.

Altruism can be crucial to the success of many business ventures. An entrepreneur may require a team of people who, besides doing their own work, also share their specialized knowledge with one another. Any bonuses awarded for helpfulness would be awfully arbitrary: Information on the exact benefit of the shared information would not generally be obtainable. An altruistic team spirit is important, even indispensable.

So altruism is a resource having valuable uses: In many business situations it has benefits for everyone in society. And various moral precepts outside the business world—"killing is wrong"—produce great social gain.

But there are situations in which an action taken in the spirit of altruism would have a perverse effect. It could do some good and no widespread harm if a firm raises pay rates in the name of a "living wage"—provided the firm is acting alone. But when all firms raise their pay, ways to economize on labor are likely to be found. Some workers will receive the higher pay, and some will lose their job and then receive no pay at all. Unemployment will rise.

A similar objection can be raised to Gates's call for greater corporate altruism and, more generally, to the growing demands for a society that tasks businesses—owners, employees, or both—with "social responsibility."

Before I get to this objection, I want to comment on some

libertarian objections of the Chicago school, which I can share only up to a point. One can agree with the libertarians that most of us would flourish less, even suffer, if we had to live in a society in which we were told what to do with our time, our business positions, and our wealth. And any diversion of this sort might hit businesses harder than individuals, since it is harder for a large corporation to hide the fact that it is behaving "irresponsibly" than for a single tax cheat to skip his 1040. But what if these diversions of corporate life envisioned by CSR were only on Fridays or only on Friday afternoons? What if a lot of people actually enjoyed the change of direction?

The libertarians answer that even if no one saw his personal growth stunted by companies that adopt CSR, imposing social responsibilities is wrong in principle: It is a deprivation of freedom that is as wrong as any tyranny. (It doesn't excuse a tyranny that it may not have hurt anyone.) I think this goes too far. I am more pragmatic than that. On the other hand, I would not go so far as to say that it is all right of society to pressure or legally coerce businesses to meet "social responsibilities" as long as that has the "consent of the governed." That would take us down the road to corporatism.

I prefer the stance taken by John Rawls, the most important political and moral philosopher America has had. He would not have seen any injustice in asking for specified corporate social responsibilities, provided such responsibilities were approved by all—including, of course, the least advantaged participants in the economy, the lowest earners. He would have said it was important that our society confer on us the political liberty to enact laws (and, presumably, to erect ethical requirements) but only those consonant with the notions of justice imbedded in our constitution.

The other objection from the Chicago school asks why, if people want to send vaccines and mosquito nets to areas suffering under acute poverty, it would not be superior to make individual charitable donations rather than call upon businesses to (in essence) tax labor and capital with the cost of carrying out social responsibilities. Well, one reason is that group efforts are more satisfying than individual ones. An employee working on a company's social contribution has the gratification of knowing that other employees are contributing too; I bet employees and investors would contribute more than they would acting alone. A second answer, discussed by some other contributors, is that individuals and charities generally lack the specialized knowledge and resources that businesses have.

A similar answer can be used in response to a question that comes from the left: Instead of calling for business altruism, why not raise taxes and use the additional revenue to subsidize public health goods and other antipoverty interventions? Well, the most plausible answer is that the U.S. government does not have the information and expertise that doing many such things requires; businesses do. So perhaps it is better to call on companies to exercise social responsibility directly rather than to tax them and subsidize other efforts.

That said, problems of information could create serious pitfalls for corporate responsibility programs. Conventionally, the innovators behind a new product, the entrepreneurs that develop the product, and the capitalists that finance it have an incentive to confine their efforts to the directions believed to be profitable—and, almost by definition, it is the profitable innovations that are best received by the public. The innovators who do not think hard about what the market wants will, in the absence of dumb luck, lose money. In contrast, there is no analogous market discipline that pushes companies to donate the right kinds of vaccines and develop the right kinds of socially beneficial technologies—in Esther Duflo's words, there is no automatic feedback loop. And the likely consequence is that socially responsible companies will not be quick and astute in correcting their mistakes. Even in a competitive market, it is difficult for a firm to infer where it went wrong with a particular good or service. How much more difficult it must be when there is no market-tested evidence that the vaccine or technology supplied was not the best one! Self-interests within a company may dictate continued production and development of ill-chosen projects—even if it is better to innovate badly in areas of great need than innovate well in areas of great plenty.

Information problems could also cause corporate programs to have perverse effects. Decades ago I saw *Heavens Above!*, starring Peter Sellers, in which an Anglican vicar is assigned to an English town, where he preaches the gospel of charity. But the unanticipated consequence of the charity was to drive another town into mass unemployment. (The solution in the movie was to reassign the vicar to outer space, where he could do no harm.) The point is this: There is always a risk that American firms, if they flood impoverished regions with new technologies and various other goods, will drive out of business other firms—including indigenous ones—that were already in the business of meeting local needs.

A final difficulty with using corporate philanthropy to remedy social problems is that, since the CSR programs are all voluntary, participating may result in the loss of competitive edge. As the share prices of philanthropic firms drop, capital will tend to desert them. And if American firms as a whole become more philanthropic, some capital will find a new home abroad.

Altruism is a hugely valuable resource. A society that has large reserves of it is able to thrive in situations where there would otherwise be difficulties. But enlisting people's altruism to serve philanthropic programs at corporations may sometimes lead to the undesirable side effects I have discussed here—and, no doubt, to others. So, as we contemplate harnessing altruism in the corporate world, we would do well to recall the old Chinese proverb: Be careful what you wish for.

ALTRUISTS ARE LIKE SADOMASOCHISTS
Richard Posner

I wish in closing to emphasize how little corporate phil anthropy (the practical meaning of "creative capitalism," a terrible expression that implies that nonaltruistic capitalism is uncreative) is actually philanthropic, in the sense of being driven by altruism rather than by profit maximization. Selling "fair-trade coffee," as Starbucks does to those customers willing to pay a premium for it, is not corporate philanthropy. It's just supplying a product at the profit-maximizing price to a person who is an altruist. Business is happy to sell to altruists, just as it is happy to sell to selfish people. Selling "fair-trade coffee" is no different, from the corporation's standpoint, from selling leather clothes to sadomasochists. Likewise with Nike's efforts to improve working conditions in its foreign plants: It is an example not of corporate philanthropy but of a corporate response to consumers' demand for a different production method. The hybrid car is a similar example, though the principal pitch is to the consumer's desire to spend less on gasoline rather than to his desire to reduce global warming.

"Socially responsible investment" is the same animal: If an investor wants to pay more (adjusting for risk and return) for a "fair-trade" portfolio, portfolio managers will be happy to oblige. And the employee who works for a below-market wage for a "socially responsible" employer is just like the socially responsible investor: He buys social responsibility from the firm in the form of a lower return on his human capital. That is not corporate philanthropy; it is employee philanthropy. But I wonder what exactly he gets for his contribution. If he gives up $1,000 in annual wages, does this mean that the corporation contributes $1,000 to charity (or equivalent good works)? If it's less, he is being cheated.

When these and other examples of faux corporate philanthropy are subtracted, how much genuine corporate philanthropy—managers' responding to the altruistic desires of their shareholders—is left? Little, I suspect. (One problem is that shareholders are unlikely to agree on the amount or objects of their corporation's charitable giving.) The mistake made by the advocates of creative capitalism is to attribute a discretionary choice ("Shall we be selfish or altruistic?") to a corporation when it is merely responding to its consumers and its suppliers, or its regulators. Corporate management would not need a single altruistic molecule in order to do the things grandly lauded as "creative capitalism."

There are, moreover, examples of so-called corporate philanthropy that are not only profit maximizing (which is fine), but also quite possibly pernicious, which is not fine. A current example is the oil companies' pretense to be "green" by sponsoring research on clean fuels. These claims are intended to rebuff calls for effective public regulation of carbon emissions.

It is perfectly rational for the oil companies to try to fend off such regulation, and opposition to regulation is often in the public interest because regulation is often bad. In this case, it seems to me that regulation would be good. But that is a detail. The point is that the greening of the oil companies has absolutely nothing to do with philanthropy.

WHAT GATES REALLY MEANS

Martin Wolf

Like most economists, I find the notion that we need a creative form of capitalism somewhat peculiar, particularly from the most successful—and, arguably, one of the most ruthless—capitalists of the past three decades. How can a man who played such a big role in the development of today's information technology industries believe that capitalism is not creative? Creation and—as Joseph Schumpeter remarked—destruction are what capitalism does.

So what is Mr. Gates trying to say? My interpretation comes down to just two simple points: first, capitalism is more innovative, more flexible, and, indeed, more creative than any other system known to humanity; and, second, it cannot do anything if there is no demand. We can see needs (yes, my fellow economists, there are such things as needs, as you would discover if you were deprived of water for a few days), but, in the absence of purchasing power, these do not become demands (you might just die of thirst, instead).

Economists have an answer to even this concern. Yes, it is true that people without incomes cannot make demands in the market, but a market economy will work hard to find ways of giving them incomes. The market economy is, after all, a huge machine for exploiting and then eliminating opportunities for arbitrage. There are few bigger opportunities for arbitrage than between the costs of employing expensive workers in rich countries and cheap workers in poor ones (as CNN's Lou Dobbs points out). So, in time, markets will find ways of bringing work to poor workers, thereby providing them with incomes.

Unfortunately, this can be a painfully slow process, particularly when there are billions of potential workers. It is slow because there are many obstacles to exploiting the opportunities to employ the poor: Many of them are uneducated and suffer from disease; the infrastructure needed to bring what they produce to the market is inadequate; and, for perfectly obvious reasons, the governments of countries full of poor and uneducated people tend to be incompetent, if not downright predatory.

So what we need is to find imaginative ways of doing two things: accelerating the speed with which poor people come to earn incomes; and substituting for the demand they lack, while taking advantage of the unique capacities of the market system. This, in a nutshell, is what development assistance should be about. It is surely what Mr. Gates, in his new persona as head of the world's biggest and most dynamic foundation, should be trying to do. And, as he remarks, we need to be very creative.

So what might be the solutions? Well, one, recommended by C. K. Pralahad, is to look more closely at the markets even the very poor might be able to offer. Another is to examine the possibilities for stimulating incomes and demands through microfinance. Muhammad Yunus won a Nobel Prize for this idea.

Yet these ideas are not going to be enough. So what else might there be?

Recognition is the solution, suggests Mr. Gates. Yes, recognition works rather well. It must be a powerful motivation for the creation of a foundation like his. In the U.K., he would have been put in the House of Lords, instead. The recognition accorded to philanthropists is the biggest reason for their role in the U.S. So the philanthropist receives recognition and the poor obtain the benefits of the demand for services generated by his money.

Yet recognition is not going to be enough to move companies, unless they gain tangible benefits from the activities. Microsoft obviously gains from giving software away cheaply in poor countries. It also gains from improving its image around the world through the innovative activities listed in the speech. Microsoft, moreover, has earned supernormal profits for a very long time, which has made it rather easy for the firm to be (or appear to be) relatively generous. The same, no doubt, is true of drug companies. But this is certainly not true of all or—I would argue—even most companies. Mr. Gates draws too much from his experience at Microsoft.

Some of the ways Mr. Gates envisages providing the absent demand are pretty disturbing. The idea of giving a drug company priority review of another drug in return for developing a treatment for a neglected disease is an example.

Overall, however, this is a useful approach to thinking about development assistance. It leads to a general question, namely, how to combine such assistance—be it from private or public sources—with capitalist incentives. Some implications of that question seem obvious: More aid could be given directly to people rather than via often corrupt and inefficient governments, thereby allowing them to make their own decisions on how to spend the money; more aid could take the form of prizes for solving specific problems; more aid could take the form of public-private partnerships; and more aid could be used to stimulate the development of markets and market-friendly institutions.

In short, my view is that what Mr. Gates is talking about has little to do with capitalism as a system but a great deal to do with promoting development. For those who do not believe that all you need is laissez-faire, that makes Gates's proposal an interesting, albeit incorrectly labeled, contribution.

WHAT WOULD ADAM SMITH DO?

Clive Crook

In his speech at Davos, Bill Gates quoted the opening lines of Adam Smith's *Theory of Moral Sentiments*:

> *How selfish soever man may be supposed, there are evidently some principles in his nature, which interest him in the fortunes of others, and render their happiness necessary to him, though he derives nothing from it, except the pleasure of seeing it.*

Bill doubtless meant this as a reply to those fond of quoting selectively from the other Adam Smith, author of *Wealth of Nations*. People who say they admire that book are especially keen on this sentence:

"It is not from the benevolence of the butcher, the brewer, or the baker, that we expect our dinner, but from their regard to their own interest."

Bill is telling us that even Smith—"the father of capitalism . . . who believed strongly in the value of self-interest for society"— praised the impulse to altruism. Society needs both, and this is where creative capitalism comes in. Its aim is to marry sentiment and self-interest; to unite, as it were, the two Adam Smiths.

I agree that Smith is badly served by many of his supposed followers. The idea that "greed is good," which one often sees attributed to him, is a travesty. He was no libertarian either. His idea of "natural liberty" was almost the opposite of what it is usually taken to mean (namely, "do as you wish"). He was at pains in both books to emphasize the importance of self-control, of regard for the opinions of others, and of an expansive role of government in providing security, rule of law, and economic infrastructure. Way ahead of his time, he was even in favor of compulsory schooling.

But I think it is wrong to regard *Moral Sentiments* as somehow at odds with *Wealth of Nations,* which seems to be the prevailing view. You quote one or the other, according to taste, but never both. Smith certainly saw no rift. The two books, though written with different purposes (*Wealth of Nations* to sway legislators, *Moral Sentiments* more to guide and inform a wider educated public) were a single intellectual project and fit together comfortably. Of the two, by the way, *Wealth of Nations* takes the dimmer view of "merchants"—paradoxically, since this is the title favored by free-enterprise types. *Moral Sentiments,* name-dropped mainly by the left, is kinder toward men of business, because it wants to establish the civilizing effects of commerce. What a difference it would make if anybody actually read these books.

Smith believed that most people are self-interested and sympathetic and wish to be well thought of. Successful commercial societies, he argued, are built on these traits. The question is, how can they best be combined? In modern terms, how can institutions and incentives shape, channel, and balance these sometimes conflicting instincts to promote greater peace and prosperity? This is the subject of both books.

In *Wealth of Nations,* addressed to rulers, Smith exalts competition as the way to keep self-interest in check and to subordinate producers to consumers. That is why the book is so opposed to protecting monopolies and, above all, barriers to trade. In *Moral Sentiments,* he puts less weight on public policy and more on the wellsprings of virtue. He underlines the need for the approval of others, not just as an end in itself but also as a requirement for flourishing in commercial society. In short, competition disciplines producers (*Wealth of Nations*); commercial interaction nurtures propriety and prudence (*Moral Sentiments*). These are different perspectives, but by no means contradictory.

What would Smith, cited so freely by both sides, have made of the modern corporate social responsibility debate? I am sure about one thing. He would have disagreed with Bill that a new kind of capitalism is needed to marry sentiment and self-interest. This is exactly what ordinary profit-seeking commerce achieves, in Smith's telling. This is the overarching idea in both books.

Of course, you can reject the cod-philosophical gestures of the Davos speech and still conclude that CSR is a good thing. Smith might well have done so. He was ever a pragmatist, suspicious of thinkers who like their principles cut, dried, and few in number. I cannot imagine him saying that CSR is always a good thing, or always bad. That would be very un-Smithian. He would say it depends. It usually does.

As a general matter, it would be true to the spirit of *Moral Sentiments* to say that owners of businesses should attune their conduct to the good opinion of mankind. But note that I say "owners," not managers. Who knows what Smith would have thought of twenty-first-century corporate governance? The modern corporation is a form he could barely have envisaged.

As a relentless advocate of ethical conduct, he might say that managers are trustees and owe their first duty to the owners of the assets under their control. In that case, doing good works at the expense of profits to seek "recognition" (as Bill advocates) would be straightforwardly unethical. On the other hand, he might observe that modern shareholders are not really "owners" at all: they have limited liability and accept little or no responsibility for the firm's conduct. Managers carry that burden, and their concerns for "stakeholders" (over and above what maximum profits require) are therefore, arguably, ethically legitimate.

The debate over the rights and wrongs of CSR is usually cast as a question about the duties of the corporation. But a lot of our disagreement, I think, boils down to a narrower question: What are, or should be, the duties of managers with respect to shareholders? Do we prosper best if we oblige managers to act strictly as agents or if we indulge their desire to act as owners? I say the first. I don't know what Smith would say.

PUTTING CREATIVITY BACK INTO CREATIVE CAPITALISM

John Quiggin

Although the conversation here takes place under the banner of "creative capitalism," there has been relatively little discussion of creativity in the ordinary sense of the term. Yet the relationship between creativity and capitalism has rarely been more complex and interesting than it is today.

The central technical innovation of the past twenty years or so has been the rise of the internet, and particularly the various incarnations of the World Wide Web. Without the internet and the web it is unlikely that we would have seen any significant recovery from the productivity growth slowdown of the 1970s and 1980s.

Yet neither the internet nor the web was a product of the market economy, and even now the relationship between market incentives and the social contribution made by internet-related activities is tenuous at best.

Both the internet and the web were developed as noncommercial activities, outstripping or absorbing a variety of commercial competitors (Genie, Delphi, AOL, and so on) before being opened up to commercial use in the mid-1990s. And even since large-scale commercial involvement began, most of the exciting innovation continues to come from noncommercial users (blogs and wikis, for example) or from noncommercial content producers (YouTube, Flickr, and so on). By contrast, heavily funded commercial innovations such as push technology and portals have failed or declined into insignificance.

The dominant driver of the internet economy is not profit-seeking innovation but individual and collective creativity. Creativity is, and always has been, driven by a wide range of motives, some altruistic and others, like the desire to display superior skill, rather less so. Trying to tie all of these motives to direct monetary rewards is futile and, if pushed too far, counterproductive.

Of course, corporations still have a large role to play in the economy of the internet. A company like Google, for example, provides services that cannot easily be replicated by users acting either individually or collectively. But Google depends crucially and directly on the content created by users and, more generally, on the goodwill of the internet community.

If these assets were lost, Google would be vulnerable to displacement; Microsoft's loss of its seemingly unassailable dominance of both personal computing and the internet software market is an illustration. Google's slogan "Don't be evil" and its sensitivity to criticism—for example, over its compliance with Chinese censorship laws—shows that Google needs, or at least badly wants, society's approval. So do the many products Google creates and gives away, with no obvious path to future profit.

So, more than in the past, it makes sense for corporations to cultivate diffuse goodwill, rather than focusing solely on profit, perhaps tempered slightly by the need to buy off powerful interests. In the context of an economy where creative collaboration is central, this can't be done through a neat separation of targets and instruments, with a charitable PR effort bolted onto a profit-maximizing corporation.

Extending all of this to the challenge of helping poor countries creates further challenges. Companies will need to do more than bring corporate expertise to bear on the development problem. They will also need to mobilize contributions of skills and resources from outside the company. If such contributors are not to feel exploited and abused, the project can't be directly tied to the goal of profit maximization. All this may yet be a bridge too far.

Richard Posner recognizes much of this but argues that corporate managers should instead adopt a hypocritical pose of general concern until they have secured a user base large enough to be locked in, and then exploit it to maximize profits. There are several problems here. First, sincerity is not as easy to fake as all that, particularly in an organization, where you can't let everyone in on the joke. Second, setting up a monopoly by stealth, then extracting the maximum rent is a trick that can be pulled off at most once. Finally, if the managers of a company are chosen to be capable of successfully conning the public in the interests of shareholders, why would anyone expect them to forgo the chance to enrich themselves at shareholders' expense?

APPENDIX

A few items originally published elsewhere that relate to this dis-cussion of creative capitalism

THE SOCIAL RESPONSIBILITY OF BUSINESS
Milton Friedman

From The New York Times Magazine, *September 13, 1970. Copyright © 1970 by The New York Times Company.*

When I hear businessmen speak eloquently about the "social responsibilities of business in a free-enterprise system," I am re-minded of the wonderful line about the Frenchman who dis-covered at the age of seventy that he had been speaking prose all his life. The businessmen believe that they are defending free enterprise when they declaim that business is not concerned "merely" with profit but also with promoting desirable "social" ends; that business has a "social conscience" and takes seriously its responsibilities for providing employment, eliminating dis-crimination, avoiding pollution, and whatever else may be the catchwords of the contemporary crop of reformers. In fact, they are—or would be if they or anyone else took them seriously— preaching pure and unadulterated socialism. Businessmen who talk this way are unwitting puppets of the intellectual forces that have been undermining the basis of a free society these past decades.

The discussions of the "social responsibilities of business" are notable for their analytical looseness and lack of rigor. What does it mean to say that "business" has responsibilities? Only people can have responsibilities. A corporation is an artificial person and in this sense may have artificial responsibilities, but "business" as a whole cannot be said to have responsibilities, even in this vague sense. The first step toward clarity in examining the doctrine of the social responsibility of business is to ask precisely what it implies for whom.

Presumably, the individuals who are to be responsible are businessmen, which means individual proprietors or corporate executives. Most of the discussion of social responsibility is directed at corporations, so in what follows I shall mostly neglect the individual proprietors and speak of corporate executives.

In a free-enterprise, private-property system, a corporate executive is an employee of the owners of the business. He has direct responsibility to his employers. That responsibility is to conduct the business in accordance with their desires, which generally will be to make as much money as possible while conforming to the basic rules of the society, both those embodied in law and those embodied in ethical custom. Of course, in some cases his employers may have a different objective. A group of persons might establish a corporation for an eleemosynary purpose—for example, a hospital or a school. The manager of such a corporation will not have money profit as his objective but the rendering of certain services.

In either case, the key point is that, in his capacity as a corporate executive, the manager is the agent of the individuals who own the corporation or establish the eleemosynary institution, and his primary responsibility is to them.

Needless to say, this does not mean that it is easy to judge how well he is performing his task. But at least the criterion of performance is straightforward, and the persons among whom a voluntary contractual arrangement exists are clearly defined.

Of course, the corporate executive is also a person in his own right. As a person, he may have many other responsibilities that he recognizes or assumes voluntarily—to his family, his conscience, his feelings of charity, his church, his clubs, his city, his country. He may feel impelled by these responsibilities to devote part of his income to causes he regards as worthy, to refuse to work for particular corporations, even to leave his job, for example, to join his country's armed forces. If we wish, we may refer to some of these responsibilities as "social responsibilities." But in these respects he is acting as a principal, not an agent; he is spending his own money or time or energy, not the money of his employers or the time or energy he has contracted to devote to their purposes. If these are "social responsibilities," they are the social responsibilities of individuals, not of business.

What does it mean to say that the corporate executive has a "social responsibility" in his capacity as businessman? If this statement is not pure rhetoric, it must mean that he is to act in some way that is not in the interest of his employers. For example, that he is to refrain from increasing the price of the product in order to contribute to the social objective of preventing inflation, even though a price increase would be in the best interests of the corporation. Or that he is to make expenditures on reducing pollution beyond the amount that is in the best interests of the corporation or that is required by law in order to contribute to the social objective of improving the environment. Or that, at the expense of corporate profits, he is to hire "hard-core" unemployed instead of better qualified available workmen to contribute to the social objective of reducing poverty.

In each of these cases, the corporate executive would be spending someone else's money for a general social interest. Insofar as his actions in accord with his "social responsibility" reduce returns to stockholders, he is spending their money. Insofar as his actions raise the price to customers, he is spending the customers' money. Insofar as his actions lower the wages of some employees, he is spending their money.

The stockholders or the customers or the employees could separately spend their own money on the particular action if they wished to do so. The executive is exercising a distinct "social responsibility," rather than serving as an agent of the stockholders or the customers or the employees, only if he spends the money in a different way than they would have spent it.

But if he does this, he is in effect imposing taxes, on the one hand, and deciding how the tax proceeds shall be spent, on the other.

This process raises political questions on two levels: principle and consequences. On the level of political principle, the imposition of taxes and the expenditure of tax proceeds are governmental functions. We have established elaborate constitutional, parliamentary, and judicial provisions to control these functions, to assure that taxes are imposed so far as possible in accordance with the preferences and desires of the public—after all, "taxation without representation" was one of the battle cries of the American Revolution. We have a system of checks and balances to separate the legislative function of imposing taxes and enacting expenditures from the executive function of collecting taxes and administering expenditure programs and from the judicial function of mediating disputes and interpreting the law.

Here the businessman—self-selected or appointed directly or indirectly by stockholders—is to be simultaneously legislator, executive, and jurist. He is to decide whom to tax by how much and for what purpose, and he is to spend the proceeds—all this guided only by general exhortations from on high to restrain inflation, improve the environment, fight poverty, and so on and on.

The whole justification for permitting the corporate executive to be selected by the stockholders is that the executive is an agent serving the interests of his principal. This justification disappears when the corporate executive imposes taxes and spends the proceeds for "social" purposes. He becomes in effect a public employee, a civil servant, even though he remains in name an employee of a private enterprise. On grounds of political principle, it is intolerable that such civil servants—insofar as their actions in the name of social responsibility are real and not just window-dressing—should be selected as they are now. If they are to be civil servants, then they must be elected through a political process. If they are to impose taxes and make expenditures to foster "social" objectives, then political machinery must be set up to make the assessment of taxes and to determine through a political process the objectives to be served.

This is the basic reason why the doctrine of "social responsibility" involves the acceptance of the socialist view that political mechanisms, not market mechanisms, are the appropriate way to determine the allocation of scarce resources to alternative uses.

On the grounds of consequences, can the corporate executive in fact discharge his alleged "social responsibilities"? On the other hand, suppose he could get away with spending the stockholders' or customers' or employees' money. How is he to know how to spend it? He is told that he must contribute to fighting inflation. How is he to know what action of his will contribute to that end? He is presumably an expert in running his company—in producing a product or selling it or financing it. But nothing about his selection makes him an expert on inflation. Will his holding down the price of his product reduce inflationary pressure? Or, by leaving more spending power in the hands of his customers, simply divert it elsewhere? Or, by forcing him to produce less because of the lower price, will it simply contribute to shortages? Even if he could answer these questions, how much cost is he justified in imposing on his stockholders, customers, and employees for this social purpose? What is his appropriate share and what is the appropriate share of others?

And, whether he wants to or not, can he get away with spending his stockholders', customers', or employees' money? Will not the stockholders fire him? (Either the present ones or those who take over when his actions in the name of social responsibility have reduced the corporation's profits and the price of its stock.) His customers and his employees can desert him for other producers and employers less scrupulous in exercising their social responsibilities.

This facet of "social responsibility" doctrine is brought into sharp relief when the doctrine is used to justify wage restraint by trade unions. The conflict of interest is naked and clear when union officials are asked to subordinate the interest of their members to some more general purpose. If the union officials try to enforce wage restraint, the consequence is likely to be wildcat strikes, rank-and-file revolts and the emergence of strong competitors for their jobs. We thus have the ironic phenomenon that union leaders—at least in the US—have objected to Government interference with the market far more consistently and courageously than have business leaders.

The difficulty of exercising "social responsibility" illustrates, of course, the great virtue of private competitive enterprise—it forces people to be responsible for their own actions and makes it difficult for them to "exploit" other people for either selfish or unselfish purposes. They can do good—but only at their own expense.

Many a reader who has followed the argument this far may be tempted to remonstrate that it is all well and good to speak of Government's having the responsibility to impose taxes and determine expenditures for such "social" purposes as controlling pollution or training the hard-core unemployed, but that the problems are too urgent to wait on the slow course of political processes, that the exercise of social responsibility by businessmen is a quicker and surer way to solve pressing current problems.

Aside from the question of fact—I share Adam Smith's skepticism about the benefits that can be expected from "those who affected to trade for the public good"—this argument must be rejected on grounds of principle. What it amounts to is an assertion that those who favor the taxes and expenditures in question have failed to persuade a majority of their fellow citizens to be of like mind and that they are seeking to attain by undemocratic procedures what they cannot attain by democratic procedures. In a free society, it is hard for "evil" people to do "evil," especially since one man's good is another's evil.

I have, for simplicity, concentrated on the special case of the corporate executive, except only for the brief digression on trade unions. But precisely the same argument applies to the newer phenomenon of calling upon stockholders to require corporations to exercise social responsibility (the recent GM crusade, for example). In most of these cases, what is in effect involved is some stockholders trying to get other stockholders (or customers or employees) to contribute against their will to "social" causes favored by the activists. Insofar as they succeed, they are again imposing taxes and spending the proceeds.

The situation of the individual proprietor is somewhat different. If he acts to reduce the returns of his enterprise in order to exercise his "social responsibility," he is spending his own money, not someone else's. If he wishes to spend his money on such purposes, that is his right, and I cannot see that there is any objection to his doing so. In the process, he, too, may impose costs on employees and customers. However, because he is far less likely than a large corporation or union to have monopolistic power, any such side effects will tend to be minor.

Of course, in practice the doctrine of social responsibility is frequently a cloak for actions that are justified on other grounds rather than a reason for those actions.

To illustrate, it may well be in the long-run interest of a corporation that is a major employer in a small community to devote resources to providing amenities to that community or to improving its government. That may make it easier to attract desirable employees, it may reduce the wage bill or lessen losses from pilferage and sabotage or have other worthwhile effects. Or it may be that, given the laws about the deductibility of corporate charitable contributions, the stockholders can contribute more to charities they favor by having the corporation make the gift than by doing it themselves, since they can in that way contribute an amount that would otherwise have been paid as corporate taxes.

In each of these—and many similar—cases, there is a strong temptation to rationalize these actions as an exercise of "social responsibility." In the present climate of opinion, with its widespread aversion to "capitalism," "profits," the "soulless corporation," and so on, this is one way for a corporation to generate goodwill as a byproduct of expenditures that are entirely justified in its own self-interest.

It would be inconsistent of me to call on corporate executives to refrain from this hypocritical window-dressing because it harms the foundations of a free society. That would be to call on them to exercise a "social responsibility"! If our institutions, and the attitudes of the public make it in their self-interest to cloak their actions in this way, I cannot summon much indignation to denounce them. At the same time, I can express admiration for those individual proprietors or owners of closely held corporations or stockholders of more broadly held corporations who disdain such tactics as approaching fraud.

Whether blameworthy or not, the use of the cloak of social responsibility, and the nonsense spoken in its name by influential and prestigious businessmen, does clearly harm the foundations of a free society. I have been impressed time and again by the schizophrenic character of many businessmen. They are capable of being extremely farsighted and clearheaded in matters that are internal to their businesses. They are incredibly shortsighted and muddleheaded in matters that are outside their businesses but affect the possible survival of business in general. This shortsightedness is strikingly exemplified in the calls from many businessmen for wage and price guidelines or controls or income policies. There is nothing that could do more in a brief period to destroy a market system and replace it by a centrally controlled system than effective governmental control of prices and wages.

The shortsightedness is also exemplified in speeches by businessmen on social responsibility. This may gain them kudos in the short run. But it helps to strengthen the already too prevalent view that the pursuit of profits is wicked and immoral and must be curbed and controlled by external forces. Once this view is adopted, the external forces that curb the market will not be the social consciences, however highly developed, of the pontificating executives; it will be the iron fist of Government bureaucrats. Here, as with price and wage controls, businessmen seem to me to reveal a suicidal impulse.

The political principle that underlies the market mechanism is unanimity. In an ideal free market resting on private property, no individual can coerce any other, all cooperation is voluntary, all parties to such cooperation benefit or they need not participate. There are no values, no "social" responsibilities in any sense other than the shared values and responsibilities of individuals. Society is a collection of individuals and of the various groups they voluntarily form.

The political principle that underlies the political mechanism is conformity. The individual must serve a more general social interest—whether that be determined by a church or a dictator or a majority. The individual may have a vote and say in what is to be done, but if he is overruled, he must conform. It is appropriate for some to require others to contribute to a general social purpose whether they wish to or not.

Unfortunately, unanimity is not always feasible. There are some respects in which conformity appears unavoidable, so I do not see how one can avoid the use of the political mechanism altogether.

But the doctrine of "social responsibility" taken seriously would extend the scope of the political mechanism to every human activity. It does not differ in philosophy from the most explicitly collectivist doctrine. It differs only by professing to believe that collectivist ends can be attained without collectivist means. That is why, in my book *Capitalism and Freedom,* I have called it a "fundamentally subversive doctrine" in a free society, and have said that in such a society, "there is one and only one social responsibility of business—to use its resources and engage in activities designed to increase its profits so long as it stays within the rules of the game, which is to say, engages in open and free competition without deception or fraud."

WHAT'S SO BAD ABOUT POVERTY?

Richard Posner

Here is Richard Posner's assessment of Bill Gates's Davos speech, from the Becker-Posner Blog of February 10, 2008.

I became acquainted with Bill Gates when some years ago I mediated (unsuccessfully) the Justice Department's antitrust suit against Microsoft. I was reassured to discover that the world's wealthiest person is extremely intelligent and surprisingly unpretentious. But I am disappointed by the recent speech on "creative capitalism" that he gave at the World Economic Forum in Davos last month.

Almost half the world's population is extremely poor, subsisting on less than $2 a day; a billion are thought to subsist on less than $1 a day. Most of the very poor live in sub-Saharan

Africa and in southern Asia. Gates argues that the key to alleviating their poverty is "creative capitalism," whereby private firms in the United States and other wealthy countries seek both profits and "recognition" (praise) in serving the needs of the poor, for example, by developing technologies designed specifically for their benefit. C. K. Prahalad, a business school professor admired by Gates, notes that Microsoft is "experimenting in India with a program called FlexGo, where you prepay for a fully loaded PC. When the payment runs out, the PC shuts down, and you prepay again to restart it. It's a pay-as-you-go model for people with volatile wages who need, in effect, to finance the purchase."

If there are good business opportunities in poor countries, however, it does not require Gates's urging for businesses to seek to exploit them. So the only meat in his concept of creative capitalism is his proposal that businesses accept subnormal monetary returns in exchange for getting a good reputation as do-gooders. But if a reputation for good works has cash value, then, once again, there is no need for Gates to urge businesses to serve the poor; self-interest will be an adequate motivator. If it is true as he says in his speech that "recognition enhances a company's reputation and appeals to customers; above all, it attracts good people to the organization," then creative capitalism pays because it enables a firm to charge higher prices to its customers and pay lower quality-adjusted wages to its employees. Whether this is true of a given firm's customers and employees is something that the firm is better able to gauge than an outsider, even so distinguished a one as Bill Gates.

If, on the other hand, reputation does not have cash value, or enough cash value to offset the reduction in financial returns that would result from conducting one's business in such a manner as to obtain a reputation for altruism, then the motivation for creative capitalism would have to be businessmen's feeling good about helping the disadvantaged. But which businessmen—corporate managers or investors? Do shareholders— the corporation's owners—feel good when corporate management picks objects of charity, unless the charitable giving feeds the bottom line (as when a firm makes charitable donations to activities and institutions in the places in which it has its plants or offices)? Unless shareholders are eager to see their corporations give massive amounts to charities that are chosen not by the shareholders but by management and that do not contribute to corporate profits, it is hard to see how urging businesses to be disinterestedly charitable can have a significant effect. A business that fails to maximize profits places itself at a competitive disadvantage relative to businesses that do maximize profits. Only if charity contributes to profits is it a plausible investment for an investor-owned firm.

There is a hint in Gates's speech that profit maximization is the real goal, and the question for "recognition" a veneer. When he talks up "business models that can make computing more accessible and more affordable," it sounds as if he may be trying to develop new markets for Microsoft. That is also the implication in Prahalad's statement that I quoted. Gates talks about "markets that are already there," that is, in poor countries, "but are untapped." In other words, there are business opportunities in poor countries, and business opportunities require imagination rather than altruism to exploit.

A curious omission in Gates's speech is a theory of why so many people are desperately poor. When he says that "diseases like malaria that kill over a million people a year get far less attention than drugs to help with baldness," he does not pause to inquire why that is so. It is so, first of all, because people in wealthy countries do not suffer from malaria, and, second, because cheap but highly effective methods of combating malaria, such as mosquito netting and indoor spraying of DDT (which would have few negative environmental effects, unlike outdoor spraying), are somehow not provided, but for reasons political and cultural rather than financial. We know that a nation doesn't have to be rich in natural resources to be prosperous. The essential ingredient of economic growth is human capital, and it depends primarily on the existence of a political system that prevents violence, enforces property rights, provides a minimum level of public goods, and minimizes governmental interference in the economy. Without such institutions, economic growth will be stunted; altruistic capitalists will not cure their absence.

Gates has discovered the Adam Smith of *The Theory of Moral Sentiments,* where Smith argued that people are not purely self-interested, but instead are actuated, to a degree anyway, by altruism. But modern studies of altruism find it concentrated within the family and trace it back to the "selfish gene"—helping someone who shares one's genes may increase the spread of those genes in subsequent generations, and if so there will be natural selection for a degree of altruism. And so as the relationship between people attenuates because of distance, race, and other factors, the degree of altruism declines. That is one reason that Gates's argument that "recognition enhances a company's reputation and appeals to customers; above all, it attracts good people to the organization" falls short. Few customers will pay more, and few skilled workers will accept lower wages, to benefit poor people in distant lands.

Finally, I take issue with Gates's assumption that alleviating world poverty is an unalloyed social good. He calls himself an optimist, but some might describe him as a Pangloss, when he says that "the world is getting better" and will be better still if there are no more poor people. If Gates said that prosperity, longevity, and other good things have increased in most of the world, he would be right. But there is no basis for predicting that these trends will continue, given such threats to peace and prosperity as international terrorism, political instability, nuclear proliferation, and global warming. And if creative capitalism does succeed in lifting billions of people out of poverty, the problem of global warming will become even graver than it is because the world demand for fossil fuels will soar.

COMPANIES AS CITIZENS

Michael Kinsley

This is a piece on corporate social responsibility that I wrote twenty-one years ago for The Wall Street Journal. *I include it out of vanity and because I think it still holds up pretty well. Juanita Kreps was commerce secretary in the Carter administration. William Coleman was secretary of transportation under LBJ and still, in 1987, a leading African-American member of the Great and the Good.*

(Copyright © 1987, Dow Jones & Co., Inc.)

The American corporation comes under attack in two new books, both of which accuse it of lacking "responsibility." But what the authors have in mind by that term reflect very different images of what social and economic role the corporation ought to play.

From the left, or thereabouts, comes *Rating America's Corporate Conscience: A Provocative Guide to the Companies Behind the Products You Buy Every Day,* a team effort by the

Council on Economic Priorities (Addison-Wesley, $14.95 paper). Anyone who wishes to lug this fat tome to the supermarket can look up which brand of "non-dairy dessert whip" is made by the firm least involved in defense contracting, what firms have the best employee day-care arrangements, and so on. From the right, or thereabouts, comes *Boone,* the memoir of Texas takeover artist T. Boone Pickens Jr. (Houghton-Mifflin, $18.95). Mr. Pickens styles himself the avatar of the interests of the small shareholder, and ends his book with a plug for United Shareholders of America (USA—geddit?), a would-be mass shareholders lobby Mr. Pickens founded last year, which you can join for a mere $50.

The CEP's standards for "corporate responsibility" are: share of profits donated to charity; number of women and minorities among top officers and on boards of directors; willingness to disclose "social information" to nosy groups like the CEP; involvement in South Africa; conventional- and nuclear-weapons contracting, and PAC contributions.

Many *Wall Street Journal* readers, of course, will disagree with these criteria. They might wish to buy their non-dairy dessert whip from the company that is doing more, not less, to strengthen America's defenses in a dangerous world. The authors, I think, would say: Fine, if those are your priorities. Their overarching concept is one of "corporate citizenship": the corporation as a political institution that should be dealt with as such. Others, who share the council's general political slant, will find some of its criteria laughably beside the point. Will the world really be a better place if Juanita Kreps and William Coleman snare a few more fat directors' fees while Henry Kissinger snares a few less? Who cares?

But differing criteria aside, is it really a good idea to turn the economy into one huge secondary boycott? If consumers decide which brand of peanut butter to buy based on social and political criteria, it stands to reason that they will have to sacrifice economic criteria to some extent. They will either pay more or get worse peanut butter. Or, if there is no real price or quality competition among peanut butters anyway, shouldn't that be of even greater concern to the Council on Economic Priorities?

In short, isn't the CEP misunderstanding the nature of capitalism, a system whose basic structure it does not challenge? The proper social role of the corporation is to produce the best peanut butter at the lowest price, leaving to individuals and to the political system such matters as support for the arts and how much we spend on defense. There's a lot to be said, even from a left-wing viewpoint, for the idea that corporations should keep to their own sphere and not attempt to become all-embracing social-service agencies.

In particular, I am not impressed by corporate charity and cultural benefaction, which amount to executives playing Medici with other people's money. You wouldn't know, from the lavish parties corporate officers throw for themselves whenever they fund an art exhibit or a PBS series, that it's not costing them a penny. The shareholders, who aren't invited, pick up the tab for the parties, too. There's a catch-22 logic behind corporate charity, which the CEP seems to endorse: It's good for the corporate image to be thought charitable; a good image is good for profits (the CEP will urge people to buy your peanut butter); therefore corporate charity is a justifiable expenditure of shareholders' money. But if it's actually a hard-nosed business decision, why give the corporation credit for generosity? In which case the syllogism unravels.

Mr. Pickens's vision of the corporation is not as a free-floating social and political entity, but as a simple mechanism through which shareholders collectively maximize their profits. When he talks about corporate abuses, he means inept or greedy management, not dumping toxic wastes or closing factories. In fact, the ruthless rationalization he and his fellow raiders have forced on company after company has turned them away from exactly the sort of "soft" considerations for which the Council on Economic Priorities awards points.

Mr. Pickens is a phony in many ways. His "barefoot boy from Texas versus the Wall Street slicksters" routine is a joke. His suits are as expensive as any, he has a vast public-relations apparatus, and he travels with a praetorian guard of special assistants. Despite his denials, he has taken greenmail, which is hardly a service to the 47 million American stockholders with average incomes of $37,000 whom he claims to represent. But he does represent a theory of the corporation that is more right than wrong. If you believe in capitalism, then you have to believe that the main social function of the corporation is to maximize its own profits in the production of goods and services, which the companies the raiders target have sometimes failed to do.

It's not quite as simple as the raiders and their defenders would have you believe, though. Shareholders are not just shareholders. We are all bundles of interests: We want a profit on our shares, we want clean air and water, we want a just society. Yet the Pickens theory slices off and maximizes just one interest. There is something a little crazy—not rational at all—about some bow-tied young investment banker in New York taking steps that will force a company to shut down a plant in the name of "maximizing value for the shareholders," when the shareholders might include the pension fund for the workers in that very plant, or other workers getting the same treatment from another investment banker down the street. Political action committees and lobbyists protect our interests as corporate shareholders far better than we can protect our political interests in less-organized aspects of our lives. The net result may or may not reflect the true political interests of people who happen to own shares, let alone people in general.

Apart from pure self-interest, the corporate system leads us to act as shareholders in ways we never would act as individuals. Most of us don't try to squeeze every penny out of life. A sole proprietor of a family firm in a small town can sacrifice profits out of sentimental pride in product or community concern in ways that could land a big corporate executive with a shareholder derivative suit, or at least have him looking over his shoulder to see if Boone Pickens or Carl Icahn was coming along to rationalize his hide.

I wouldn't want either Boone Pickens or the Council on Economic Priorities running my corporation.

GOOD COMPANY

Clive Crook

This is a 2005 essay by Clive Crook in The Economist *that takes on many of the ideas raised by creative capitalism. Reprinted with permission.*

Over the past ten years or so, corporate social responsibility (CSR) has blossomed as an idea, if not as a coherent practical program. CSR commands the attention of executives everywhere—if their public statements are to be believed—and especially that of the managers of multinational companies headquartered in

Europe or the United States. Today corporate social responsibility, if it is nothing else, is the tribute that capitalism everywhere pays to virtue.

It would be a challenge to find a recent annual report of any big international company that justifies the firm's existence merely in terms of profit, rather than "service to the community." Such reports often talk proudly of efforts to improve society and safeguard the environment—by restricting emissions of greenhouse gases from the staff kitchen, say, or recycling office stationery—before turning hesitantly to less important matters, such as profits. Big firms nowadays are called upon to be good corporate citizens, and they all want to show that they are.

On the face of it, this marks a significant victory in the battle of ideas. The winners are the charities, nongovernment organizations, and other elements of what is called civil society that pushed for CSR in the first place. These well-intentioned groups certainly did not invent the idea of good corporate citizenship, which goes back a long way. But they dressed the notion in its new CSR garb and moved it much higher up the corporate agenda.

In public-relations terms, their victory is total. In fact, their opponents never turned up. Unopposed, the CSR movement has distilled a widespread suspicion of capitalism into a set of demands for action. As its champions would say, they have held companies to account, by embarrassing the ones that especially offend against the principles of CSR, and by mobilizing public sentiment and an almost universally sympathetic press against them. Intellectually, at least, the corporate world has surrendered and gone over to the other side.

The signs of the victory are not just in the speeches of top executives or the diligent reporting of CSR efforts in their published accounts. Corporate social responsibility is now an industry in its own right, and a flourishing profession as well. Consultancies have sprung up to advise companies on how to do CSR, and how to let it be known that they are doing it. The big auditing and general-practice consulting firms offer clients CSR advice (while conspicuously striving to be exemplary corporate citizens themselves).

Most multinationals now have a senior executive, often with a staff at his disposal, explicitly charged with developing and coordinating the CSR function. In some cases, these executives have been recruited from NGOs. There are executive-education programs in CSR, business-school chairs in CSR, CSR professional organisations, CSR websites, CSR newsletters and much, much more.

But what does it all amount to, really? The winners, oddly enough, are disappointed. They are starting to suspect that they have been conned. Civil-society advocates of CSR increasingly accuse firms of merely paying lip service to the idea of good corporate citizenship. Firms are still mainly interested in making money, they note disapprovingly, whatever the CEO may say in the annual report. When commercial interests and broader social welfare collide, profit comes first. Judge firms and their CSR efforts by what the companies do, charities such as Christian Aid (a CSR pioneer) now insist, not by what they say—and prepare to be unimpressed.

By all means, judge companies by their actions. And, applying that sound measure, CSR enthusiasts are bound to be disappointed. This year's Giving List, published by Britain's *Guardian* newspaper, showed that the charitable contributions of FTSE 100 companies (including gifts in kind, staff time devoted to charitable causes, and related management costs) averaged just 0.97 percent of pretax profits. A few give more; many give almost nothing (though every one of them records some sort of charitable contribution). The total is not exactly startling. The figures for American corporate philanthropy are bigger, but the numbers are unlikely to impress many CSR advocates.

Still, you might say, CSR was always intended to be more about how companies conduct themselves in relation to "stakeholders" (such as workers, consumers, the broader society in which firms operate and, as is often argued, future generations) than about straightforward gifts to charity. Seen that way, donations, large or small, are not the main thing.

Setting gifts aside, then, what about the many other CSR initiatives and activities undertaken by big multinational companies? Many of these are expressly intended to help profits as well as do good. It is unclear whether this kind of CSR quite counts. Some regard it as "win-win," and something to celebrate; others view it as a sham, the same old tainted profit motive masquerading as altruism. And, even to the most innocent observer, plenty of CSR policies smack of tokenism and political correctness more than of a genuine concern to "give back to the community," as the Giving List puts it. Is CSR then mostly for show?

It is hazardous to generalize, because CSR takes many different forms and is driven by many different motives. But the short answer must be yes: For most companies, CSR does not go very deep. There are many interesting exceptions—companies that have modeled themselves in ways different from the norm; quite often, particular practices that work well enough in business terms to be genuinely embraced; charitable endeavors that happen to be doing real good, and on a meaningful scale. But for most conventionally organized public companies—which means almost all of the big ones—CSR is little more than a cosmetic treatment. The human face that CSR applies to capitalism goes on each morning, gets increasingly smeared by day, and washes off at night.

Under pressure, big multinationals ask their critics to judge them by CSR criteria, and then, as the critics charge, mostly fail to follow through. Their efforts may be enough to convince the public that what they see is pretty, and in many cases this may be all they are ever intended to achieve. But by and large, CSR is at best a gloss on capitalism, not the deep systemic reform that its champions deem desirable.

Does this give cause for concern? On the whole, no, for a simple reason. Capitalism does not need the fundamental reform that many CSR advocates wish for. If CSR really were altering the bones behind the face of capitalism—sawing its jaws, removing its teeth and reducing its bite—that would be bad: not just for the owners of capital, who collect the company's profits, but, as this survey will argue, also for society at large. Better that CSR be undertaken as a cosmetic exercise than as serious surgery to fix what doesn't need fixing.

We are an equal-opportunity employer

But this is not the end of the matter. Particular CSR initiatives may do good, or harm, or make no difference one way or the other, but it is important to resist the success of the CSR idea—that is, the almost universal acceptance of its premises and main lines of argument. Otherwise, bones may indeed begin to snap and CSR may encroach on corporate decision making in ways that seriously reduce welfare.

Private enterprise requires a supporting infrastructure of laws and permissions, and more generally the consent of electorates, to pursue its business goals, whatever they may be. This is something that CSR advocates emphasize—they talk of a "license to operate"—and they are quite right. But the informed consent of electorates, and an appropriately designed economic infrastructure, in turn require an understanding of how capitalism best works to serve the public good. The thinking behind CSR gives an account of this which is muddled and, in some important ways, downright false.

There is another danger too: namely, that CSR will distract attention from genuine problems of business ethics that do need to be addressed. These are not in short supply. To say that CSR reflects a mistaken analysis of how capitalism serves society is certainly not to say that managers can be left to do as they please, nor to say that the behavior of firms is nobody's concern but their own. There is indeed such a thing as "business ethics": managers need to be clear about that, and to comprehend what it implies for their actions.

Also, private enterprise serves the public good only if certain stringent conditions are met. As a result, getting the most out of capitalism requires public intervention of various kinds, and a lot of it: taxes, public spending, regulation in many different areas of business activity. It also requires corporate executives to be accountable—but to the right people and in the right way.

CSR cannot be a substitute for wise policies in these areas. In several little-noticed respects, it is already a hindrance to them. If left unchallenged, it could well become more so. To improve capitalism, you first need to understand it. The thinking behind CSR does not meet that test.

CONTRIBUTORS

ABHIJIT BANERJEE is the Ford Foundation International professor of economics at MIT.

GARY BECKER is the university professor of economics and sociology at the University of Chicago. He was awarded the Nobel Prize for economics in 1992.

JAGDISH BHAGWATI is a university professor of economics at Columbia University.

NANCY BIRDSALL is the founding president of the Center for Global Development.

MATTHEW BISHOP is the chief business writer and American business editor of *The Economist* magazine.

WARREN BUFFETT is the chairman and CEO of Berkshire Hathaway.

KYLE CHAUVIN is a student of economics and math at Harvard University.

GREGORY CLARK is a professor of economics at the University of California, Davis, and the author of *A Farewell to Alms*.

CONOR CLARKE is a fellow at *The Atlantic Monthly* and a former editor at *The Guardian*.

CLIVE CROOK is the Washington columnist for the *Financial Times* and a writer for *National Journal* and *The Atlantic Monthly*.

JOSH DANIEL is the senior advocacy officer at the Bill & Melinda Gates Foundation.

MICHAEL DEICH is the deputy director of public policy and external affairs at the Bill & Melinda Gates Foundation.

J. BRADFORD DELONG is a professor of economics at the University of California, Berkeley, and a research associate of the NBER.

ESTHER DUFLO is the Jameel Professor of Poverty Alleviation and Development Economics at MIT.

WILLIAM EASTERLY is a professor of economics at New York University and a senior fellow at the Brookings Institution.

JUSTIN FOX is the business and economics columnist for *Time* magazine.

ALEXANDER FRIEDMAN is the chief financial officer of the Bill & Melinda Gates Foundation.

MILTON FRIEDMAN was at the time of his death in 2006 a senior research fellow at the Hoover Institution.

BILL GATES is the founder and chairman of Microsoft and the Bill & Melinda Gates Foundation.

RONALD GILSON is a professor of law and business at both Stanford and Columbia law schools.

ED GLAESER is a professor of economics and director of the Taubman Center for State and Local Government at Harvard University.

TIM HARFORD is a *Financial Times* columnist and author of *The Undercover Economist*.

MICHAEL KINSLEY is a columnist for *Time*, past editor of *The New Republic* and *Harper's*, editorial and opinion editor of the *Los Angeles Times*, American editor of *The Economist*, and founding editor of *Slate*. His writing has also appeared in *The New Yorker*, *The Washington Post*, and other publications.

NANCY KOEHN is the James E. Robison Professor of Business Administration at Harvard Business School.

MICHAEL KREMER is the Gates Professor of Developing Societies at Harvard University.

STEVEN LANDSBURG is a professor of economics at the University of Rochester and a columnist for *Slate*.

THIERRY LEFEVBRE is a financial consultant for an international financial software editor.

LORETTA MICHAELS is a partner and cofounder of HMS Wireless.

MATT MILLER is a senior fellow at the Center for American Progress and author of *The Tyranny of Dead Ideas*, which will be published in January 2009.

PAUL ORMEROD is the founding director of Volterra Consulting and the author of three books about economics.

EDMUND PHELPS is a professor of political economy at Columbia University. He was awarded the Nobel Prize in economics in 2006.

RICHARD POSNER is a judge for the Court of Appeals for the Seventh Circuit and senior lecturer at the University of Chicago Law School.

JOHN QUIGGIN is a professor of economics and political science at the University of Queensland.

ROBERT REICH is a professor of public policy at the University of California, Berkeley, and a former secretary of labor under President Clinton.

JOHN ROEMER is the Elizabeth S. and A. Varick Stout Professor of Political Science and Economics at Yale University.

VERNON SMITH is a professor of economics and law at Chapman University. He was awarded the Nobel Prize in economics in 2002.

ELIZABETH STUART is a senior policy adviser for Oxfam International in Washington, D.C.

LAWRENCE SUMMERS is a university professor of economics at Harvard University and a secretary of the Treasury under President Clinton.

DAVID VOGEL is a professor at the Haas School of Business of the University of California, Berkeley, and editor of the *California Management Review*.

ERIC WERKER is an assistant professor at the Harvard Business School.

TRACY WILLIAMS is a policy analyst at the Bill & Melinda Gates Foundation.

JOHN WILLIAMSON is a senior fellow at the Peterson Institute.

MARTIN WOLF is associate editor and chief economics commentator at the *Financial Times*.